I0585251

Henry Cottrell Rowland

Across Europe in a Motor Boat

Henry Cottrell Rowland

Across Europe in a Motor Boat

ISBN/EAN: 9783954272327
Erscheinungsjahr: 2012
Erscheinungsort: Bremen, Deutschland

© *maritimepress in Europäischer Hochschulverlag GmbH & Co. KG, Fahrenheitstr. 1, 28359 Bremen. Alle Rechte beim Verlag und bei den jeweiligen Lizenzgebern.*

www.maritimepress.de | office@maritimepress.de

Bei diesem Titel handelt es sich um den Nachdruck eines historischen, lange vergriffenen Buches. Da elektronische Druckvorlagen für diese Titel nicht existieren, musste auf alte Vorlagen zurückgegriffen werden. Hieraus zwangsläufig resultierende Qualitätsverluste bitten wir zu entschuldigen.

Leaving Varna.

ACROSS EUROPE IN A MOTOR BOAT

A CHRONICLE OF THE ADVENTURES OF THE MOTOR
BOAT *BEAVER* ON A VOYAGE OF NEARLY SEVEN
THOUSAND MILES THROUGH EUROPE BY
WAY OF THE SEINE, THE RHINE, THE
DANUBE, AND THE BLACK SEA

BY

HENRY C. ROWLAND

AUTHOR OF "IN THE SHADOW,"
"THE WANDERERS," ETC.

ILLUSTRATIONS BY

HERBERT DELAND WILLIAMS

D. APPLETON AND COMPANY
NEW YORK   1908

CONTENTS

LIST OF ILLUSTRATIONS

vii

LIST OF ILLUSTRATIONS

viii

LIST OF ILLUSTRATIONS

ACROSS EUROPE
IN A MOTOR BOAT

ACROSS EUROPE IN A MOTOR BOAT

CHAPTER I

THE *BEAVER*

THE long water trail which those must follow who make the voyage from New York to Havre does not, as most people take for granted, stop finally at this latter port. Instead, it leads far on, past Rouen and Paris, past Strassburg and Manheim and Regensburg, on still past Vienna and Budapest and eastward where the great Danube finds its outlet in the brackish waters of the Black Sea.

It is a peculiar route, this long, wet trail across the continent of Europe, and one that only a few have ever followed throughout its course. It winds up against the current of swift rivers and twists through tortuous canals; here climbing, climbing, through endless locks it mounts from the level of one high plateau to that above it, until the air grows rare and fine, and the nights, even in midsummer, are cold.

Then down again it goes, crossing bridges which span wide rivers and through long, inky tunnels where the water is Styxlike and the roar of the engine threatens to bring down the mountain through which one burrows. Down, on down, through locks descending the mountains in a flight of watery stairs.

Rivers again; swift, treacherous rivers beset with shoals and rocks and traffic, and swinging bridges set like traps for the unwary in which one would need be caught but once. Then the canal again and locks which climb up and over a mountain range, descending on the farther side to join a lovely, rushing stream which five hundred miles below becomes a wonderful, majestic river, sweeping through yet a thousand miles of hills and forests, mountains and plain, until at last it debouches its turbid waters into the Black Sea.

Such is the water trail from Havre across the continent of Europe. Though little known, a number of adventurous spirits have already taken it. But it was to follow it throughout its course and then to hold right on, and with the same vessel to take the sea trail beyond, circumnavigating southern Europe and so returning to the starting point, that we built the *Beaver* ánd sailed out from London to face what Fortune held in store for us in a circuit of nearly seven thousand miles.

There is an old, time-worn Yankee story of a trapper who was relating to a " tenderfoot " a tale of how his dog was just about to grab a giant beaver which had pulled out of a trap when the animal scrambled up the bank and climbed a tree.

" But hold on ! " said the " tenderfoot." " You know as well as I do that a beaver can't climb a tree ! "

" Stranger," said the old man, solemnly, " them o' yourn is trew words. But *this* here beaver jes' natchully *had* to climb a tree ! "

With this tale in mind, before our boat was ever laid down in the yard we had named her the *Beaver*, because she just naturally had to do what the chances were so very much against her doing.

Briefly, this was our proposed itinerary:

Starting from London, to cross the Channel to Havre, ascend the Seine to Paris, where it is joined by the Marne, ascend the Marne to its junction with the *Marne au Rhin Canal*, follow the canal to Strassburg and thence enter and descend the Rhine to where it receives the river Main at Mainz, ascend the Main to Frankfort and there enter the ancient Ludwig Canal. Passing through the Ludwig Canal, to enter the Danube at Regensburg (Ratisbon), and to descend the Danube throughout its fifteen hundred miles of navigation to its mouth at Sulina. Thence to lay a course across the lower end of the Black Sea for the entrance of the Bosporus and pass through the Bosporus, Sea of Marmora, and the Dardanelles into the Mediterranean. Then, depending on the advancement of the season, to return coastwise to Cette, near Marseilles, and pass through the Midi Canal and thence up and around the French coast to Havre, or to pass through the Straits of Gibraltar and return by sea.

The shortest route planned describes a circuit of about eleven thousand and odd kilometers or about six thousand eight hundred and fifty miles.

The suggestion for this interesting jaunt came to me from Mr. Sanford B. Pomeroy, an American artist living in Paris. In his studio one day as we were discussing small-boat cruising, Pomeroy, who is a veteran yachtsman, remarked:

" Don't you think that it would be interesting to get a small, light-draught motor boat and go

4

straight across to the Black Sea and then return through the Mediterranean?"

"Very," I answered, and asked him what sort of wheels he would need for the boat.

"Only one," said he, "under the stern. All that you would need would be the screw and a paraffin marine motor. It is wet all of the way. A friend of mine, M. Stock of Paris, took his launch, the *Isle des Loups*, across last year."

"You will also need some sails," said I, "if you want me to go with you across the Black Sea. But why a paraffin motor? They smell."

"The smell," said my friend, "is not nearly so disagreeable as the price that we should have to pay for petrol anywhere east of Pest. Besides, there are lots of places on the route where we could not get petrol, and one can always get petroleum. There are long stretches on the lower Danube where they have never even heard of petrol and where the people would say their prayers to a motor car."

These few simple words excited me, and from this point of departure our plans proceeded rapidly. In fact, they grew with such flamboyant exuberance that I was presently forced to remark that while the idea was fascinating, we did not have the money. Pomeroy retorted that there were a great many more interesting obstacles to be overcome than the vulgar lack of funds.

" Besides," said he, " perhaps it cannot be done at all, and then we shall not need the money."

There was reason in this, so we ignored the pecuniary problem and proceeded with that of the boat. After much study of the route and information obtained from M. Stock, we came to the conclusion that we required a thirty-five-foot paraffin (petroleum) motor boat with a speed of not less than nine statute miles an hour and a draught of not over two and a half feet when running slowly. Also, she must be an able sea boat and have a cabin which would sleep three. She would also require auxiliary sail power.

But it was one thing to know what we wanted and another to get it. We could not afford to build, and being thoroughly familiar with the types of French boats, both on the coast and upon inland waters, we knew that there was small chance of finding what we needed in France. So we crossed to England and spent several days in combing the yards of Southampton and Cowes, but in vain.

" We shall have to build," said Pomeroy.

6

"We have neither the time nor the money," I objected.

"As to the time," said Pomeroy, "we shall be too late for the water to float us up the Main, and just in time to strike the equinoctial gales in the Black Sea. This will only lend added interest to the trip. But if you are going to talk about money we might as well chuck the whole thing right now, and be everlastingly disgraced in 'the Colony.'"

That settled it. Better theft, a flat car, and drowning in the Black Sea than to disappoint the Colony. We had given it out that we were going, and there would be no place for us in Paris after the end of June. Build we must, but in order to spend as little as possible of the money which we did not have we decided to design for ourselves a boat which could not cost so much to build.

Accordingly, the studio became a draughting room, Pomeroy being the draughtsman and I the consulting naval constructor. The result was a thirty-five foot boat of the "skipjack" type designed for, first, economy, second, speed, third, safety. We put safety last because we could not see how a skipjack with a maximum draught of two and one half feet and the scant beam necessary to give her speed enough to shove her against a swift river current could possibly be much of a life-boat.

These plans we sent to Messrs. Linton Hope and Company, of London, with a letter explaining the situation. In a few days we received an answer to the effect that Mr. Hope's conscience would not permit of his building such a death trap for three men to get drowned in, and strongly advising us to give up the skipjack type of boat. He expressed great interest in our project and offered to build us the proper boat for the work at a special price. Inclosed, he sent us the plans for a splendid thirty-five-foot launch of the Admiralty stock design. This boat was driven by a fourteen-horse-power paraffin internal-combustion motor, the "Dan," constructed by the Jorgensen Motor Works of Copenhagen, and was the motor in use *par excellence* by the fishermen of Scandinavia, as well as by many of the fishermen of Great Britain and Finistère.

As this boat was of a stock design and therefore a marketable commodity, we decided that at the end of the voyage Linton Hope and Company would no doubt be able to sell her at nearly what she would cost us, and accordingly we sent in our

order to build, with a time limit set for her com-
pletion and delivery to us in London.

"And now," said Pomeroy, "it is all settled.
We have got everything but the money."

Among the many extras to be considered which
were not included in the estimate for the boat itself was the dinghy. Being under the necessity
of economizing at every point, we decided that,
while the *Beaver* was being constructed in Limehouse at King's Yard, we would employ our otherwise idle moments in the construction of the dinghy
in the studio on the rue des Sablons. Accordingly,
we went around to a joiner's shop on the rue
Pétrarque, picked out our material and had it sent
around to the studio.

We had already asked a mutual friend to accompany us, Mr. A. N. Ranney, an American
resident of Paris, and he had accepted in some
doubt as to the actuality of our enterprise. On
arriving one morning at the studio and finding the
place turned into a shipyard, with the work of boat
building proceeding "full bore," his doubts van-
ished, and before long he was demonstrating the
inherent craftsmanship which is a part of the birth-
right of every native-born American.

Poor little *Sampan*! We little thought as we

sawed and planed and hammered in the quaint
old studio, what a tragic end the little boat
was destined to have, nor how we should come
across her shattered timbers high up on a Turkish
beach!

The *Beaver* was promised for the 5th of July,
so the last of June I closed my apartment in Paris
and crossed to England to superintend her com-
pletion. On arriving in London, Captain Spooner,
of the firm of Linton Hope and Company, took me
down to see the boat which was building in Limehouse. Although I had seen her several weeks
earlier, having crossed with Pomeroy to look her
over, I was very much surprised to find what a
big, stanch vessel she had grown to be.

" She may starve you, but she will never drown
you," said Captain Spooner, and weeks afterwards
his words came back to me.

The *Beaver* was certainly a love of a boat. Captain Saunders, her builder, pointed with pride to
her picked materials: Norway pine side planks all
of one piece throughout her length without a butt;
an American elm keel, a magnificent stick of timber; bent frames of the same stuff, light, strong,
and sound. Her cabin house was of teak and her
stem and stern-transom of oak. We had stipu-

The *Beaver* going overboard at Limehouse, London.

lated for a Sampson-post forward in case it should be necessary to take a tow, and there it stood—a stick of wood by which she might have been swung clear of the water.

There were certain features which I did not like. One was the absence of any decking abaft the cabin house, making her an open boat from amidships, but the limited space about the engine and cockpit made this obligatory. The arrangement of the stearing gear struck me as very faulty, the tiller lines passing through five leads in all before reaching the wheel, but try as we might we could devise no way of remedying this objection, which was destined to result in some very dangerous situations. On the whole, however, the *Beaver* was a fine, big, able boat and " all boat under water," as the saying is, with full bilges below the water line which furnished a remarkable stability and counteracted the great weight of the motor.

The first time that I saw our engine I asked, quite innocently:

" What is that thing for, a drogher or a Thames barge? "

" Dan," as our engine was named, was a two-cylinder paraffin motor which, according to some peculiar Danish system of calculation, was rated sixteen horse power, and in my opinion was nearer twenty-five, and he weighed a ton and a half! Captain Amundson had Dan's twin in his ship when he made the Northwest Passage, and he ran for a solid week without once stopping the motor. It was always hard to stop Dan, once he got well going.

Dan was a brute any way that you took him, but he was a rough, open, honest sort of a brute, once you learned his ways. His system bore the same analogous relations to that of an automobile engine that the system of a gorilla bears to the human species, but it was " simplified " by the absence of carburetor and electric ignition. The first explosion was produced by heating the ignition chambers by means of blast lamps, and, once started, the repeated combustions sustained the requisite heat for those subsequent, while the work of the carburetor was done by automatic air-inlet valves.

Nothing could be simpler, more effective, or heavier. As a commercial engine I know of nothing better than Dan, but he was about as well fitted to the *Beaver* as a truck horse would be to a basket phaeton. If I were to cruise in remote waters far from machine shops and mechanisms and fuel stations where only certain excellent brands could be obtained, I should want Dan aboard; but he would be down below in solitary confinement in a padded cell, where he could growl and swear and slam without driving nervous people to distraction. I, for my sins, was destined to be his keeper, and we always hated each other.

Dan occupied the best part of the *Beaver*, a little abaft the beam, and he was encased in a galvanized iron box, constructed to keep you from getting at him, and with two heavy, semicircular lids like the tops of round-backed trunks, and so arranged that when opened in a sea way they could come down with sufficient force to amputate your arm or fracture your spinal cord. Dan boasted two big fly wheels, one fore, one aft, which might have weighed, at a guess, three hundred pounds apiece; and he was equipped with automatic water circulation, automatic fuel pump, governor, throttle, and clutch. It took about ten minutes' heating with the blow pumps to heat him hot enough to start, and he could be stopped entirely for about ten minutes and started again without the lamps. It was a better policy, however, to keep the lamps going when it was necessary to stop the motor for several minutes.

The propeller was two-bladed, reversible, and very strong and simple in construction. The forward, neutral, and reverse angle of the blades was easily controlled by a wheel on the same axis and abaft the steering wheel, and these two worked coordinately with the throttle and clutch, both of which were within easy reach, and gave the man at the wheel perfect control of the boat which could be handled like an automobile. With a strong wind in any quarter she could be held in any desired position, turned in her length, and laid alongside without cracking an egg.

But Dan, the malignant *deus ex machina*,

needed every bridle, check, and martingale which
you could put upon him. He was a brute—a
morose, grumbling, growling, swearing, powerful,
hard-working, economical brute—and we always
hated each other! He belonged by right in the
belly of some rough-hewn, solid lump of a fisherman, and that was where he would have preferred
to be, and he never got over his disgust at being
billeted aboard a light, springy little vessel whose
supple back gave beneath the powerful downward
strokes of his heavy pistons.

The expression, " strain the motor," was a joke
as applied to Dan. You couldn't strain him; he was
far too " husky." You might strain yourself, or
the boat, or the nerves of the community which you
happened to infest, but Dan—never! He would
run without water, without lubricating oil, heat up
and swear, of course, but pound along at his 360
revolutions; he would even run without fuel if he
felt like it; on what I'm sure I don't know! I
think that he would have run on beer or absinthe
or castor oil if we had fed it to him; perhaps he
would have liked it. He never seemed to care
what brand of grease he got, but he *did* like the
night air and always " bucked up " after sunset.
When he was getting his full ration he worked

along on about a gallon an hour, at a cost, in England, of about sixpence.

But when he was running strong he let you know
it; he let you know that *he* was the one in the boat
who was doing all the work, and that he'd do it
as he d—— pleased, and that it was a sacrifice of
his strength and dignity to kick along a soft-shelled
thirty-five-foot pleasure packet without a ton of
cargo or a basket of fish aboard her. And in his
rage he would shake and hammer and pound the
poor little *Beaver* until I longed to grab up a spanner and beat in his ugly cylinder head!

Yes, he was a proper brute, was Dan, and I
hated him as much as I loved the *Beaver*, who was
a darling and deserving of better things than an
ugly dog of a square-head motor, as, for instance,
some large white sails! They were an ill-assorted
couple, but you see, Dan was really a size larger
than his younger brother for whom the *Beaver* had
been designed, and Linton Hope had given him to
us at the same price, thinking it better that we
should be a little overpowered. But to call Dan a
sixteen-horse power!—that is funny! Sixteen-wa-
ter buffalo, perhaps!

On looking the boat over it was very evident to
me that she was not going to be ready on time, and

I raised an awful howl, for every day was price-
less. The water in the Main River was falling as
the season advanced, and we had to get through
the Black Sea before the equinox. So in order to
make the interval before she was launched as disagreeable as possible for the builders, I established
myself in quarters on Bloomsbury Square, and
spent my days in Limehouse. The British boat
builder will not turn out a hurried or unfinished
job, however; twice the day was fixed for the
launching and twice postponed. The third time
that they tried to postpone it I formed a hollow
square.

" That boat goes overboard to-morrow," said I,
" if you have to finish her in diving armor! "

" Doctor," said Captain Saunders, " we are not
going to give you a half-finished job! "

" Then," said I, " you can have eleven months
to finish it, and I will go back to Paris and drink a
Pernod and wait."

That settled it; no boat, no final payment. The
Beaver went into the Thames under a ten-ton
crane. No doubt I was responsible for the week
of agony that followed when everything went
wrong, but I probably saved a fortnight at that.
I sat down and wrote to my two friends to say that

the yacht was at their disposal, the furniture moved in—for I had been fitting out—their beds turned down and pyjamas laid out, and would they kindly come over and see if anything necessary to their comfort had been overlooked? A few days later they came and wanted to know why I had not hurried things along, and complained that the pillows which I had bought were stuffed with scrap iron.

CHAPTER II

HEY did not arrive, unfortunately, in time for the maiden voyage, which occurred fifteen minutes after the *Beaver* was sopping up the Thames. Captain Spooner, Mr. Gus Saunders, and I assisted at this ceremony. A demoralized traffic from Wapping Stairs to the Houses of Parliament was also more or less involved, and proscenium boxes on London Bridge were greatly in demand.

Captain Spooner and Gus fired up. They did this generously, until the whole engine was a mass of roaring flame and the patrol boat of the Thames Conservancy came over and looked on with chilling disapproval. I regarded the operation with fear and awe, and was glad that Pomeroy was rated engineer.

Presently the blast lamps began to roar, and the audience on the wharf marched ten paces to the rear. I do not think that I have ever so much

3   19

admired the daring of two men as I did that of Gus and Captain Spooner. They did not appear to care whether they were blown up or not; in fáct, they rather seemed to covet a martyr's crown. The more burns they got the happier they became. I told myself that if this was the usual method of starting the motor I would sit on the bank behind a large tree while Pomeroy got the engine going.

Presently the flames subsided, but the alarming roar increased and volumes of nauseous smoke began to pour out of the motor. Somebody on the wharf suggested the fire boat.

" Just the paint burning off the motor," said Spooner, wiping his eyes. " Is she hot, Gus? "

Gus said that he did not think that she was, then touched something with his bare arm and used a strong Limehouse expression.

" Let's give her a few minutes more, captain," said he. " She'll start better when she's good and warm."

It seemed to me that she must be nearing the melting point, and that when she did start it would be straight up, but I held my peace and regretted not having remained on the wharf. Gus and Spooner began to run back and forth around the engine, opening and shutting things. Dan wore a sphinxlike expression which seemed to say, " Not yet, but soon."

Presently Spooner said: " Give her a turn, Gus; she's hot enough."

Gus fitted the crank and gave a lusty heave, but Dan refused to budge; would not even turn over.

" She's a little stiff," said he. " Hold down the valves, will you, doctor? "

In fear and trembling I picked up two spanners and jammed down the air-inlet valves, while Spooner tended the half-compression lever. Gus cranked and Dan began to breathe—*chow*—*chow* —*chow*! Gus cranked faster and Dan began to cough.

" Let go! " called Gus. I let go the valves. Spooner threw on the full compression.

Chug — chug — BANG!! went Dan — and stopped.

There was laughter from the wharf, and some lumper sang out:

" Give 'im t'other barrel, guv'nor, and put 'im hout o' 'is misery."

" Too much fuel," said Spooner. " She needs regulating."

Nobody denied it. A black cloud was still hanging over Limehouse Church.

"Try her again, Gus," said Spooner.

A titanic struggle ensued, for Gus was a powerful young man. Dan coughed and grunted and swore, and refused to budge. Gus paused for breath.

"She'll be all right after she turns over a few times," said he, encouragingly.

I believed him, but wondered how Gus would be after he had turned her over a few times. More than ever I wished that Pomeroy were there to see what his duties entailed.

Having rested, Gus grabbed the crank and gave a heave, and with a crash and a roar Dan was off!

Everybody looked scared but Spooner and Gus, who looked surprised. Spooner began to work the levers and Dan went into paroxysms. Spooner accelerated him and Dan brought up the artillery. Spooner slowed him until he wept like a child. Then Spooner discovered something that needed adjustment and tried to stop him. Dan refused to stop.

"Cut off the fuel, Gus," said Spooner. Gus did so and Dan began to run faster.

"Shove down the valves!" commanded Spooner. We did so and Dan began to pant heavily, but still ran on.

Thames barges.

" 'E's a willin' bloke, 'e is! " said a navvy on the wharf.

Suddenly Dan gasped and stopped. Spooner made his adjustment and Gus cranked again. Dan chugged along powerfully.

" Cast off! " called Spooner, taking the wheel. We cast off and the *Beaver* glided out into the stream. It was in the early afternoon and the traffic was at its height.

The Thames in the middle of London is not exactly the place that I should choose for making trial trips in a small motor boat; tramp steamers, ferryboats, barges, tows, dumb lighters drifting up with the swift tide—all sorts and conditions of craft weaving in and out, shooting with the swift current or swinging into their berths, maneuvering and turning and dodging one another, and congesting into solid masses under the arches of the bridges!

Into this vortex plunged the *Beaver*, Dan running unevenly and missing with both cylinders alternately and together. Spooner was working the fuel control, and as we passed a string of lighters Dan commenced to fire salutes. A barge threw up his hands in token of surrender and the crew of a towboat cheered. Dan went from bad to worse and stopped firing one cylinder altogether, and Gus, lifting the hood of the motor, discovered that

"The bargees   asked us to give them a tow."

the fuel pump was all adrift. As we charged up to London Bridge, the heart of a swarm of traffic of every sort, Dan stopped, the *Beaver* lost her steer-

age way, and we spun down upon the arch broadside on, narrowly missing the bridge pier on one
hand and bumping along the side of a lighter on
the other, while a tugboat fended us out from under the bows of her following barge with a pole.
Gus was half in and half out of the motor box,
and the swash of a passing steamer slammed down
the lid, almost breaking his back. Spooner, a sea
captain, was using " langwidge " to Dan, and I
was thinking how nice it would be to have Pomeroy and Ranney aboard.

But everybody was good-natured. The bargees
grinned and asked us to give them a tow; the tugboat captain offered to let us tie up to him until
we got the motor again, and the passenger steamers sheered out and gave us a wide enough berth
to sail upstream broadside on. Then, as the current was sweeping us down on some anchored
barges, Gus got the motor going again and we
limped along to a berth in front of Lambeth Palace, where Spooner wished to leave the boat during her trials—and ours!

The following morning Gus went down early to
make some adjustments, and had everything in
readiness to start when Spooner and I arrived.

" We will run down toward Greenwich," said

26

Spooner, "and then if the beggar knocks off we shall have the tide to bring us back."

We weighed anchor and started downstream against the young flood, and when we had reached the Tower Bridge Dan was thumping along so powerfully that Spooner began to exult.

"She's all right now, doctor," said he. "You can start for Constantinople to-morrow if you like—" and at this moment Dan was seized with a choking fit, then began to miss.

Spooner employed some nautical expressions and started to investigate. One cylinder was doing all of the work and getting very hot about it; the other was shirking and pleasantly cool, firing at times in weak, fitful explosions.

Spooner could not understand; neither could Gus. We limped along to Greenwich, where we tied up to a brig lying alongside the wall and went ashore and ate a silent and reflective meal. After lunch we went aboard, fired up again, and Dan threw out his chest and rushed back to Lambeth as if he loved the place! Spooner and Gus invented some plausible excuse for his bad behavior of the morning, and we agreed to let bygones be bygones.

Pomeroy and Ranney arrived the following

morning and wanted to know if I had everything all ready to start. I told them that everything was ready but the boat and they finally accepted my apologies. We went down to the landing, where we met the others. Gus fired up, and when everything was in readiness to start I said to Pomeroy:

"As you are to be the gray-haired engineer you might as well become familiar with your routine duties, the most interesting of which is starting the motor. Crank her."

Pomeroy, who is accustomed to cranking his eight-horse-power de Dion Bouton, picked up Dan's crank, which we might have used as an anchor had it been slightly different in shape, regarded it with some misgiving, adjusted it and gave a heave which would have lifted his motor car off the road. Dan did not budge.

"Something is holding her," said he.

"Yes," said I, "it is her weight. Look at those splendid big fly wheels and those Atlantic-liner crank shafts."

Pomeroy tried again and Dan gave him an inch or two. Much encouraged he paused to rest.

"Is she on half compression?" he asked.

We assured him that he should have every possible assistance, and held down the air-inlet valves.

In cruising trim: Pomeroy at the wheel.

Pomeroy braced his feet, gripped the crank, and heaved. With nothing to pull against but the weight of metal he got a revolution, then another. We let go the valves, but Dan did not start. A look of infinite discouragement passed over the face of the artist.

Happening to glance at the throttle I saw that the fuel was turned off.

" This is too bad," said I. " The joke is certainly on me; she was not getting any juice." I turned it on. " Now try again, and then if you cannot start her we will let Ranney have a go at it."

" I know nothing whatever about motors," said Ranney. " You had better not call on me; I might do it some harm."

" This crank is too short," said Pomeroy. " I am going to have a longer one made and then you will be able to start her with one hand. In the meanwhile I shall save my strength."

Gus started the motor. I think that Pomeroy did crank it once some time during our cruise— and then went to bed. Ranney never started it in his life. He did not own a share of the boat and was afraid that he might break the crank.

That day's trial trip was characterized by jarring off every nut on the motor, or nearly every nut. I think that Gus must have set them up with his fingers. At any rate he paid for it, as after each of our numerous stops we let him do the starting, and it was a humid day in the middle of July. Finally, seeing that he was " all in " Spooner and I lent a hand. After the motor had stopped coming apart we got another hot cylinder and tied up to the bank above Chelsea, and turned the engine over by hand more times than I like to think about to pump the water through and cool things off; an entirely unnecessary form of procedure as we afterwards discovered.

We landed at Putney for some much-needed refreshment. While sitting in the window of the pub. some strolling minstrels came along, looked up at us, stopped, struck up an air and began to sing:

> "Waltz me around again, Willy,
> Around and 'round and 'round."

I had heard the song before, but it was new to the others and became Dan's "hymn before action."

As it was then getting late we left the boat at Putney and returned to London by tram. Spooner and Pomeroy had come to the decision that all of our trouble lay in the piping of the water circulation, and Gus was instructed to make some changes. Nobody asked for Ranney's or my advice; perhaps they guessed that we were becoming prey to the conviction that what they did not know about Dan would, if printed, make a splendid handbook to give out to beginners.

That night Pomeroy and I talked matters over and decided that as the trouble, wherever it lay, was purely some error of adjustment, we might save time by taking over the boat, getting our papers, and being all ready to start as soon as Dan was. Accordingly, we made our final payment, got ship's papers from the U. S. Consulate, sent our gear aboard, stores, charts, nautical instruments, and had the boat all found and ready to start across the Channel as soon as the operation of the motor appeared to warrant the attempt, which we hoped would be upon the following day.

Our plan was to run down the river, dropping Gus at Limehouse if all went well to that point, then proceed to Greenhithe. Here Spooner was to leave us, and the following day we were to drop down with the tide, cross the Thames Estuary, and then, if we caught a good slant of wind and weather, hold right on, catching the change of tide off the North Foreland and, giving the Goodwins a wide berth, lay a course across and follow the French coast down to Hàvre.

These arrangements were made with no consideration of Dan, who resented it accordingly. We made a good start from Lambeth, and bucking the last of the flood had got down opposite the Temple landing when the *chug-chug-chug-chug* changed to *k'chug-k'chug-k'chug-k'chug*, and at the same time the water outlet began to come in spurts. The same old story, but worse, for presently the beat of the remaining cylinder weakened, became fitful, and expired, leaving us swirling around helplessly among a fleet of barges.

Spooner said forecastle words; Gus sighed deeply; Pomeroy began to look sagely into the motor; Ranney wiped some grease off his sleeve, and I got out an oar. Almost instantly we were surrounded by wherries and whitehall boats, which seemed to ooze out of the slimy crevices of the wall. They were like sea gulls fighting over a dead porpoise, or buzzards come to a dead donkey. Some actually tried to get a line to us without our consent, but Spooner talked to them in the fluent dialect of the India Docks and Gus contributed some Limehouse *bonmots*, and they sheered off. We paddled alongside a lighter and made fast.

"Well, Mr. Pomeroy," said Spooner, "what do you think of your boat?"

"She is very interesting," said the artist.

Spooner, a thoroughly good fellow and very sore about our ill luck, laughed and said: "If I

33

were the buyer and you were the seller I'm afraid that I would not take it as you do."

Pomeroy said that there was no use in taking it any other way, and told him the story of the beaver. The tale cheered him up considerably.

After some delay we succeeded in starting the motor again and crawled along downstream, our object being to find a berth where we could tie up and work at the motor without getting mashed in. The river knew us pretty well by this time, and everybody was interested and sympathetic and, seeing us crippled, gave us the right of way.. As it was evident that we could not run much longer we got over on the Wapping side and there had a very narrow escape from being crushed by the steamer *Oriole*, which was breasting into her berth. We got clear of her by about three inches and then, swirling down through a tangled meshwork of traffic of every sort, finally reached Limehouse pier, Spooner working the automatic feed pump by hand.

Immediately on making fast we were surrounded by a swarm of wharf rats, lumpers, navvies, and "bums," such as only this, the toughest part of London, can produce. Spooner scanned this mob with an experienced eye.

34

"We must keep an eye to windward with this gang," said he. "I'll pick out the toughest tough of the lot, and hire him to beat in the heads of the

London Bridge.

other toughs, or they'll be aboard and steal the keyhole out of the cabin door."

The rest of the day was spent in trying to find the source of the missing cylinders, but without success. When the others had expended their supply of technical terms I took a spanner and started to take off the forward cylinder head. They watched me in cold disapprobation.

" What do you want to do? " asked somebody.

" We will call it an explanatory laparotomy," said I.

" I wouldn't unseat that cylinder head; it has been carefully packed, and you will loosen the packing and it will all have to be done over again. What do you want to take it off for? "

I answered that although that was the cylinder which refused absolutely to work they had examined everything else about the motor and never touched the cylinder itself, which was theoretic and not practical surgery. The cylinder was suffering from a pathological condition, whether functional or organic, and I was going to look at it.

Spooner regarded me thoughtfully, then grabbed up a wrench and lent a hand. We got off the cylinder head and found the asbestos-paper packing full of water. There was also some water in the cylinder itself.

" Well, I'll be d——d! " said somebody.

I agreed with him. Here was all of this talent frittering around and spouting the jargon born of

36

the comparatively recent revolution of power in applied mechanics, yet while knowing the physiology of Dan's thermotaxic system, failing to apply it! When they read this and see how I have " exposed " them, they will be angry. I am glad of it. That is one of the objects of this article.

We were destined to have a good deal of trouble from the same source until we learned how to pack a cylinder head by soaking the asbestos paper in oil and smearing it with plumbagine. But we had found the source, as somebody expressed it, of " the whole bloody trouble."

Englishmen consider "bloody" an improper word; they also correct us for saying " bug " and for using certain other convenient generic terms. Personally, I consider " bloody " a splendid word, and " Lime'us " could not exist without it. It fills so admirably the place of every expletive adjective and adverb in the English language, and is neither obscene nor blasphemous, simply vulgar, which is often synonymous with " popular." We had an illustration of its utility that night. Spooner and I were ashore, and during our absence a local waterman came down and discovered to his rage that his wherry had been shifted to make a berth for the *Beaver*.

"I bloody calls this a bloody piece o' bloody h'impertinence!" says he, and whips out his knife and slashes at the *Beaver's* warps. Our paid protector promptly grabbed him by the throat, choked him into submission and kicked him ashore, then returned to the boat.

"Such bloody be'avior," says he to Ranney, "is werry bloody wrong, sir."

Ranney agreed and asked him the cause of the row.

"'E was bloody h'angry becuz 'is bloody boat 'ad been shifted, sir. Such conduc' is bloody h'uncalled for *and* h'upsettin'."

We three slept on the *Beaver*, and the next morning Gus repacked both cylinder heads. On firing up Dan started off with a lusty roar that bid defiance to the thousands of leagues before him. Spooner had joined us, and bidding Gus good-by we backed out into the stream and started down river. Dan churned along strongly and evenly, and it really seemed as if our troubles were over.

On reaching the measured mile we ran over the course both with and against the tide, and the average gave us a speed of nine statute miles an hour.

CHAPTER III

THAT night we lay off Greenhithe, we three sleeping aboard and Spooner returning to London. Much to our delight he said that he would try to join us the following morning for the run across the Channel. Quite aside from his business interest in the *Beaver*, Captain Spooner was too much of a sportsman to have let us start out on a run which, considering the recent performances of Dan, entailed some actual risk, without being present to share it with us. We were very glad because, aside from his being a most congenial shipmate, he knew the Thames Estuary and the Channel as he did his own quarter deck, and one cannot overestimate the value of accurate local knowledge, especially in such a stretch of water as the Estuary.

True to his word Captain Spooner joined us the next morning with the cheering news that he was free to accompany us as far as Boulogne or Dieppe. As we had missed the morning's ebb tide we spent the day in Greenhithe laying in stores and fuel. At 8.40 P.M. we got our anchor and started out, and by ten o'clock had reached the Estuary, where, as the weather conditions seemed to indicate fog for the night with an easterly blow in the morning, we decided that it would be better to put into Hole Haven for the night than to hold on across. The Thames Estuary of a thick, blowy night seemed an even less attractive place for a small, open motor boat but half tuned up than did the river itself in the heart of London.

Accordingly we ran into Hole Haven and dropped anchor in the midst of a fleet of eel boats. The next morning the weather had cleared, so we got under way and started out, but had not quite laid the Chapman abeam when the forward cylinder stopped firing.

Captain Spooner's comments went far toward counteracting the depressing influences of the situation.

" Who'd ever have thought," said he in conclusion, " that this bloomin' bombshell would serve us a pup like this ! "

But we knew now where the trouble lay, and soon had the cylinder head off and repacked, when Dan started with renewed vigor.

"We had better put into Ramsgate," said Spooner, " and get this packing job done by a professional. There is something faulty with our methods."

Dan proved the truth of these words by shortly beginning to miss with both cylinders, but he kept going, and we laid a course for Ramsgate by the " Overland Passage." We passed the Nore Light Vessel, and were beginning to look hopefully toward the North Foreland when Dan gave a grunt and stopped.

It is one thing to have your motor fail you in the Thames and another to have it do so halfway across the Thames Estuary, a body of water justly dreaded for its treacherous shoals, swift tides, fogs, and exposed to the sweep of Channel gales. There was no refuge to be had, so we examined Dan with much interest and found that not only was the cylinder packing leaking again, but a poorly soldered fuel pipe to the after cylinder had broken in the joint and was squirting the oil everywhere but into the ignition chamber; also that the fuel pump itself had worked loose again and was rocking on its bed and so lessening its thrust.

We served the fuel pipe and got it fairly tight, hardened down the loosened nuts and then started the motor, which limped along in a jaded manner, threatening every moment to stop, and often fulfilling the threat. Each time it did so we managed to start it again after a Græco-Roman struggle with the crank, and after a while the North Foreland loomed close ahead, with Ramsgate just around the other side.

" If the bloke " (this was not the word, but it will do) " will only take us around the buoy," said Spooner, " we shall be all right-O. The tide is fair on the other side."

All hands got to work at Dan, Spooner working the fuel pump by hand; the overworked cylinder was kept cool by opening the drip cock on its water jacket and plugging the water-circulation outlet, thus forcing the cold water around the hot cylinder and out into the bilge, whence one hand pumped it out with the bilge pump. So, coaxing and bullying and jockeying Dan into a final spurt for the Ramsgate breakwater, we limped around the end of the jetty, the focus of attention from an admiring Sunday crowd of picnickers.

Once inside Spooner threw the throttle wide.

" Now kick yourself alongside, you —— —— you ! " said he, and with a volley of salutes which awoke the echoes of the town, Dan churned the

Ramsgate Harbor.

43

water and expired, while the *Beaver*, holding her way across the basin, glided gracefully up to the jetty, where ready hands caught up our heaving line.

Our arrival in Ramsgate harbor was attended with a rather humorous incident. The tide was very low, and as we slid up to the sea wall a boat containing two of the harbormaster's men came alongside to give us a berth. One of them, a big, beefy fellow, wishing to get up on the wall, borrowed our boat hook and, catching it in an iron ring overhead, braced his feet against a crevice in the stones and started up, hand over hand. Almost at the top the hook broke from a flaw in the iron, and down came the sailor, landing like a ton of brick half in and half out of his boat. His mate grabbed him and hauled him aboard.

It looked to us as if the man must have broken his back, staved in all of his starboard ribs, and started some of his joints. It sounded that way, too. But he scrambled up, and the first thing he did was to examine the thwart and gunnel of his boat. Then he looked at the boat hook.

" W'y blarst me," says he, " this 'ere was the bloody thing as done it! " He turned to one of us. " It's lucky as 'ow the blighter broke now, sir,

44

not doin' no h'especial 'arm to nobody. H'otherwise it might ha' served ye a pup some d'y when
you was dependin' on it!"

We told him that we considered that he had
done us a service, at which he seemed much
pleased.

This was the twenty-first of July and a Sunday,
so that we were obliged to wait until the next
morning to get a mechanic to come aboard and
repack our cylinder heads. When he saw the
sort of asbestos paper which had been used, he
said:

" That stuff is no good. It soaks the water up
like lamp-wicking, and carries it over into the cylinder head, and if there's any one thing those engines
hate to burn, it's water!"

Dan, our motor, certainly hated it. He did
not care particularly what his liquor was, but he
liked it straight!

The professional repacked our cylinder heads
and water joints, soldered the broken fuel-feed
pipe, and by eleven o'clock we were ready for sea.
The day was cloudy with a w. s. w. wind and
showers of rain and a generally unsettled-looking
condition of the weather, but the sea was smooth,
and we had already lost so much time that we de-

termined to try for the French coast. Accordingly, we " heated up," turned over the motor, and chugged out of the breakwater.

Dan thumped along strongly and steadily, but we were careful not to comment on the fact. If I were to write a Handbook for Beginners on the running of internal-combustion engines, the initial precept would be: " Never praise the motor ! " Aboard a sailing vessel I am not superstitious; that is, not very. I don't mind capsizing a hatch cover or leaving a bucket of water standing on the deck, or being shipmates with a Baptist parson or an umbrella. In the transatlantic race for the Kaiser's Cup in 1905, I threw enough money over the taffrail to bring a gale of wind, and it did! But shipmates with a motor, and especially a motor which had shown the diabolic ingenuity which Dan had for stopping in the wrong place, I am constantly the prey to superstitious fear. Dan knew every word that was said about him; but while ugly he was at the same time subject to abuse and intimidation. Later, in the Danube, when I had learned a lot of nice, new, strong and vigorous terms of abuse, I always commenced the day by lifting the hood and showering them on Dan, and ·it kept him right up to his work. That is a good thing for the young motorist to know. The older ones all appear to have discovered it.

So we put out and laid a course through the haze for the South Foreland, and by one o'clock had laid it abeam. A little later we sighted the Channel Squadron maneuvering, and by two o'clock the mist had blown away and the day become a lovely one. We were by this time in mid-channel, and I suggested that it was an appropriate time to break out and hoist our American ensign. We had not done so earlier, owing to Dan's villainous behavior. Upon seas where an American vessel is a rare but time-honored guest we were unwilling that the *Beaver* should bring contumely upon her flag by spinning down with the tide stern first, or tied up alongside a garbage scow, or, perhaps, drag ignominiously into port behind some aromatic trawler. A sailing vessel loses nothing of her dignity by towing; a power boat does. " Yew 'ave legs—w'y doant yew stand on 'em ! " as a bargee complained one day when we, in a disabled condition, grabbed his rail.

But Dan's functional infantile complaint had now been remedied, so we got out our American ensign and mastheaded it on our British boat with its Danish motor, and pledged the good old flag in good old Scotch! It was sort of an international event. Spooner, who was a New Zealander, made a few appropriate remarks, and we took another drink to *his* flag, the one under which the *Beaver* had been launched. We would have taken still another drink to the Danish flag, in honor of Dan, but we were afraid that he would get conceited and stop, and we were in mid-channel with a boat all open abaft the cabin house, and not a rag of sail aboard. So somebody hid the whisky.

Poor little flag! The only one the *Beaver* ever owned! Many nations looked upon it; the citizens of some saw it for the first time upon their inland waters, and many people actually asked us what country's flag it was! Weeks later when I flew it for the last time—reversed—and watched the fierce gale whip it into ribbons, the picture of our first " colors " came back to me.

After " colors," Spooner made us a famous stew—an Irish one—and by the time that we were beginning to recover from the stupor following the gorge, Cape Griz Nez was looming up on our port beam and the *Beaver* made her first bow to *La belle France*, which she was destined to traverse. As it was then getting late in the day and Spooner had to start back to London the morning following, we decided to put into Boulogne for the night. On getting into the harbor we found the berth a very noisy and unquiet one, owing to the big fleet of fishermen which are constantly coming and going. So we waited until slack water and then ran into the inner basin, where we found a snug place alongside a brig, whose captain we subsidized as watchman.

As soon as we had tied up, two customs men in a small boat came alongside and asked us if we had come from America. We said: " No, we have come from England."

" But the boat must have come from America," they insisted, " because you are flying the American flag."

" That is because we are Americans, and it is our boat."

" Oh; so that is it. Whereabouts in America do you live? "

" Well, you see, although we are Americans, we live in Paris."

They couldn't make it out at all. I don't know that I blame them. Presently one of them asked:

" Where are you bound? "

" To Constantinople, then back through the Mediterranean and up the coast to Havre."

Most men in their position would have thought
.that we were lying, but they accepted our word
with such perfect faith that we explained to them
our trip, in which they were much interested. We
chatted for a while, and then one of them said:

" Oh, by the way, you haven't any contraband,
have you? "

" Only a few cigarettes for ourselves."

" That does not matter; merci, messieurs
au 'voir messieurs, bon voyage." And they bowed
and pulled away, and the terrible formality of the
customs was over.

This was the treatment which we received from
the customs all of the way: Germany, Austria,
Hungary, Servia, Bulgaria, Roumania, Roumelia,
Turkey—no one ever doubted our words. We
never did have any contraband, of course, that not
being our mission, and we told them so, and they
believed us. They looked at our flag and said:
" These are Americans and, therefore, truthful;
besides, they are our guests, and it behooves us to
treat them as such." This, at least, was the way
in which they acted. They did not ask us to swear
and then force us to submit to the insult of having
some official try to prove us liars.

Another thing which I should like to credit the

continent of Europe with in this connection is the honesty of her peoples. In crossing the continent from the Atlantic Ocean to the Black Sea, we repeatedly left the boat tied up to the bank in different rivers and canals, and entirely unguarded, at all hours of the day and night. The cabin, which contained many valuable articles, we naturally locked up, but the cockpit and engine room were entirely open and contained many articles of some value, such as tools, lanterns, oil cans, drums of petroleum and expensive lubricating oil, and coils of rope with blocks, many of which were in plain sight and in reach from the bank itself. Yet throughout the course of the whole voyage we never missed one single article. Only twice did we engage a watchman, and that was to keep the children from climbing all over the boat and, perhaps, casting off the warps, as the current was swift. In time we gained such faith in the honesty of the people that we would not even take the trouble to put articles which were apt to excite cupidity, as sheath knives, out of sight. Ranney one day dropped a bucket overboard and did not tell Pomeroy, dreading his comments on such carelessness. When Pomeroy in time missed the bucket, and was obliged to conclude that some one had stolen it, his grief over his shattered confidence and lost ideals was so great that Ranney had to confess.

Apparently these common people are just naturally and simply honest. One day, early in the voyage, I asked the friendly captain of a French canal boat if it were safe to go off and leave the boat unprotected.

" Why, perfectly," said he, in a tone of surprise.

" There is then no danger of things being taken from the boat? "

" Not at all; those things in the boat do not belong to other people; they belong to you, so naturally nobody will take them away!"

I decided that such a country was wrongly named; it should be called Altruria!

Certainly no foreign vessel was ever better treated in strange ports than was the *Beaver*. At first we wondered, then became accustomed to it, and finally, I fear, a bit spoiled by it. But such is human nature!

CHAPTER IV

N the morning Spooner came down to
see us off, and as soon as Pomeroy had
returned from the bureau of the captain of the port with our papers, we
heated Dan up, and, bidding Spooner
good-by with much regret, started out to sea. I am
sure that no yacht builders ever did more for a cus-
tomer than did Linton Hope and Company for us,
through Captain Spooner. He cheerfully shared
the trials and dangers of the harrowing days spent
in demoralizing the traffic of the Thames in London river and those of our uncertain trip across
the Thames Estuary to Ramsgate. Unsatisfied
still with the dependability of the motor he volunteered to cross the Channel with us, and would
have gone on to Havre had not positive engagements compelled his return to London.

We ran out around the buoy and had laid a
course down the coast, keeping a good offing, when
suddenly the forward cylinder began to fire fit-

fully; but by this time I had learned a few of Dan's cunning little ways, and soon had him running evenly again. Being the only one aboard who could, or would, turn the engine over, I had taken on the duties of *mécanicien*, Pomeroy being navigator, while Ranney was speedily promoted from deck hand to the billet of quartermaster, and did most of the steering.

The weather was fine, with a fresh easterly breeze; a fair wind with a following sea which helped us along considerably. As the conditions were so favorable we decided to make a run directly to Havre, and accordingly took a broad offing, and by noon had laid the Etaples Light abeam. During the day the wind backed into the north and freshened, so remembering the amount of trouble which we had had with Dan and his capacity for sulking at the critical moment, we decided to keep well offshore, which would give us time to work over the motor, if necessary to stop for any length of time, without finding ourselves up against the cliffs. Accordingly, we kept well off, sometimes losing the land as we cut across the big bights of the shore, but cutting in close again where the headlands projected. This coast is a very bold one and visible in clear weather for, perhaps, twenty miles, so that although we had no log and distrusted Dan's demoralizing influence upon our compass, there was no possibility of our losing our bearings.

Rounding Cape Alprech and much nearer to the cliffs than was pleasing to me, Dan suddenly swore and stopped. It was a very trying moment; the land was close under our lee—a *falaise* of sheer cliffs with the seas spouting high at its base; the wind had freshened and there was no shelter of any sort which we could reach. The *Beaver* lost her way, swung broadside on, and began to drift rapidly toward the shore, rolling heavily in the rising sea.

Also it was personally inconvenient, as I happened to be up forward taking a bucket shower bath, but I lost no time in getting aft and starting a rapid clinical examination of Dan. This speedily showed the fuel pump to be all adrift, the lock nuts having loosened, which permitted of its rocking on its base, thus losing the force of the stroke. It did not take long to remedy the trouble; nevertheless, we had drifted pretty well in toward the reefs before we got the nuts hardened down and the motor going again.

Such an incident is very disturbing. Before this

occurred we had put past misfortunes well back in
the lockers of our minds, and were giving ourselves
up to the pleasures of the run in open sea and the
delight of the charming marine pictures surrounding us. A loose nut and how different the inter-
pretation to the mind of every detail! The magnificent sheer cliffs bathed in mauve and purple
shadows and fringed with a lacework of flying
spray became grim, cold, and pitiless. The fresh,
invigorating north wind carried a menace in every
flaw, and each rising sea, helpmates before,
growled some surly threat as it passed. The com-
radeship we had felt for it all was turned in a
flash to combativeness, and all because a loose nut
had reminded us what we might expect of this
good-natured, helpful monster we bestrode if once
we fell beneath his power. Such a feeling rarely
comes to one aboard a sailing vessel; at any rate,
it only comes when the fight is really on and the
challenge has been offered and accepted, but it
doesn't come so traitorously in the midst of kindly
surrounding conditions.

Afterwards, we found ourselves listening constantly for the slightest change in the beat of the
motor. This alertness was quite involuntary, but
we got tired of it after a while, and decided that

as we were due to meet a strong head tide which we would have to " buck " all night long and could not in any case make very good progress, we might as well put into Dieppe and pass a comfortable night. As somebody expressed it:

" She may run right through to Havre without stopping again, but if she should stop it might be hard to find out, in the dark, what was wrong, and anyway, what's the use of getting heart disease every time she misses? "

Nevertheless, the chances are that we would have gone on just the same had we not met the incoming tide off Treport and found what very slow work it was driving into it. Also it kicked up a nasty, lumpy sea which made steering of any kind very difficult and steering a compass course almost impossible. The compass would " turn 'round and stare you in the face," as sailors say, so realizing that by keeping on we should only use up much oil and energy and gain very little time, we decided to put into Dieppe.

On arriving off the breakwater we found a very nasty condition of things for entering. At certain phases of the wind and tide a sailing vessel cannot get into Dieppe, nor for that matter could a motor boat as open as was the *Beaver*. There is a tide rip just outside the harbor mouth with a sea which runs all ways at once, while a current like a mill race strikes across the opening at right angles. If one turns in around the tideward jetty too soon there is a splendid chance of being dashed into it by a back eddy, whereas if one does not turn in soon enough the slash of the current is apt to fling the boat against the breakwater on the other side. The best way is to work up against the tide, and when just in the right position turn quickly and slip in. We accomplished it in this way without any trouble, but were obliged to get dangerously near to the rocks of either jetty. No doubt the local fishermen can go in and out at most times; in such a place local knowledge is, of course, usually able to compete with local conditions.

We sailed from Dieppe the following morning at ten. The weather was perfect, with a fresh, following wind and sea. The bright, yellow sunlight brought out magnificent effects of light and shadow in the sheer, cream-colored cliffs, the beauty of which Dan kindly permitted us to enjoy. A French torpedo boat passed us, flying to windward in a shower of spray, and several times we were able to exchange pleasantries with the gurry-

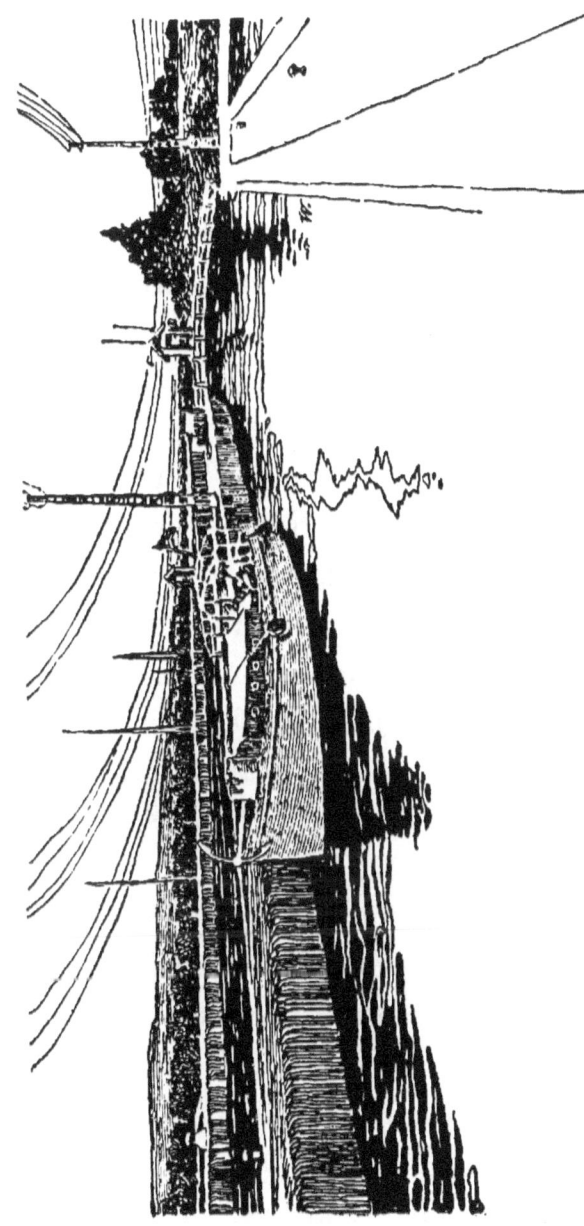

Locking through at Havre.

smeared crews of trawlers. Passing Etretat, where we had several friends, we ran in as close as we dared, which was not, however, more than near enough the shore for us to distinguish figures, as the wind was directly on the beach and there is no shelter of any sort. We learned afterwards that we had been sighted and recognized.

We arrived off Havre at about half-past four, having made the run from Dieppe, one hundred and one kilometers, in six and a half hours; poor time, considering the fair tide and wind. As the tidal conditions were unfavorable for going on up the Seine, we decided to spend the night in Havre and to save time the following morning by passing through the Tancarville Canal, which enters at Havre and cuts across the marshes of the Seine estuary for fourteen and a half miles, joining the river at Tancarville.

That night we lay in La Citadele basin, next to the wharves from which the French liners sail. The dock master informed us that we really had no business there, as it was strictly against the rules to admit internal combustion motor boats, but upon our assuring him that we burned an inexplosive compound, lamp oil, he allowed us to remain on condition that we would promise not to blow up

60

the warehouse of the Compagnie Générale Trans-
atlantique.

As Dan was such a dirty brute, we always
dressed while aboard the boat in the blue-jean costume worn by mechanics. This proved to be a
most advantageous practice, for many unanticipated reasons. European ideas of sport do not,
like ours, approve the wearing of " hard clothes."
On the Continent a sportsman is always dressed—
and usually overdressed—for the part. To a
Frenchman, particularly, the idea of three gentle-
men sportsmen doing their own work and dressed
in the blue dungaree of mechanics would be quite
incomprehensible. In fact, a gentleman would
gain no particular esteem in their eyes by merely
knowing how to do these things, the inference being that such work must at one epoch of his life
have been his calling; otherwise, how could he have
learned it? As a result, we were always assumed
to be three professionals engaged to take the boat
somewhere for the patron who was doubtless some
richard Américain. We never undeceived them.
In consequence, we were always received upon
terms of friendly equality and the people were
chatty and communicative, while a small *pourboire*
went a very long way.

Our nationalities also puzzled them. Pomeroy, from his pointed beard and perfect French accent, was always taken for a Frenchman; Ranney, who spoke German as fluently as English and had a light mustache and complexion, was usually thought to be German. I am sure I don't know what they took me for; a " Scandahoovian," perhaps, and no doubt they thought that I was a sort of under servant of the other two, being rather careless in my costume and usually bareheaded.

While lying in the basin at Havre a Frenchman came over and asked me where we had come from. When I said " London " he looked skeptical.

" Ah! You brought her on a steamer," said he.

" No," said I, " we brought her on the water. Why not? She is a boat, not an automobile."

" But you have no sails! What if the motor should not march? "

" It has to march," said I. " It is against the rules for it to stop."

He shrugged. " But I suppose," said he, " that you are very well paid for it. For me, I should want a good deal of money to cross the *Manchi* in such a *canot automobile!* "

Sometimes we were found out. Later, in the French canals Pomeroy had an amusing experience. It was at the junction of two different canal systems, and he was asked by the lock keeper to accompany him to the office of the superintendent and show his papers. Pomeroy was at the time

A lock keeper.

dressed as a neat, self-respecting *mécanicien,* and the lock keeper's manner was the least bit patronizing. They reached the office and the superintendent glanced first at the papers, then at Pomeroy.

" Pray be seated, monsieur," said he, politely.

Pomeroy thanked him and sat down. The lock keeper stared at the superintendent with an expression of astonished disgust. That this great man, the chief of the whole canal, should invite a workman to take one of his own chairs was most astounding!

The superintendent examined the papers, then suddenly paused, took out his cigarette case and offered it to Pomeroy. Pomeroy took a cigarette. The lock keeper's eyes opened wider, his mouth as well. Pomeroy took out his own cigarette case and offered it to the superintendent.

" Perhaps you would like to smoke an Egyptian cigarette," said he.

The superintendent took one, thanked him, lit a match, offered it to Pomeroy, then lit his own cigarette and proceeded with his examination of the papers. The lock keeper leaned against the wall for support. The superintendent countersigned the papers and returned them with a smile to Pomeroy.

" You are Mr. Pomeroy? " he asked.

Pomeroy admitted it, observing that the superintendent had penetrated his disguise.

" Naturally, such a costume is much more convenient," said the superintendent, " but I have yet

64

to see a *mécanicien* who wears jeweled rings while on duty, who uses the same forms of expression which you have employed, or who offers one Egyptian cigarettes from a gold case marked with his coat of arms! "

But there was never a more disgusted lock keeper on a French canal!

One must be careful to choose the right conditions of tide for ascending the lower part of the Seine, as there is a very dangerous bore or tidal wave, known as the *mascaret*, which has brought many a small vessel and some large ones to grief. This *mascaret* is caused by the first of the flood tide sweeping up the estuary and being then funneled down as the river narrows, where it meets the combined rush of the ebb tide and the river current. The result, during the periods of very high tides, is a wave across the river some four or five feet in height in the middle, but mounting in the shallows near either bank to a height of twenty or thirty feet. It travels at a speed of thirty-five to forty kilometers an hour, and is followed at intervals of a few hundred yards by three other waves. It is felt very strongly as high up as Duclair, fifty-four miles from the mouth, and then gradually dies away. At Rouen, seventy-six miles from the mouth, I noticed it as a slight ripple in the water only a few centimeters higher than the level before it.

Were a boat, even of considerable size, to be caught by the *mascaret* over the shallow water it could not possibly escape destruction, and there is a case on record of a tramp steamer which was wrecked, some of her crew being drowned. The *mascaret* never need take one unprepared, however, as the roar with which it advances is like that of Niagara. Some sailing directions we had aboard advised one caught by the approaching *mascaret* to make for deep water and then let go an anchor, paying out cable as the wave met the bow of the boat. They did not explain how one was going to lie at anchor with the boat's head toward the *mascaret* in a swift ebb tide! It sounded to me as if the person who wrote it had studied out the problem over a *Pernod* in some *café*. If we had encountered the *mascaret* we would have taken the middle of the river and headed slowly into it, under way, or if disabled, taken it as the junks do in the Yangtse Kiang, tail-to, and trusted to the stern and side curtains to act as weather clothes and keep out the wet!

The following morning we passed through the

Tancarville Canal, and on coming out into the Seine found that we had under us the last of the flood, which we carried well up beyond Caudebec. Before we had proceeded far we heard suddenly ahead of us the rattling exhaust of a rapidly run-

"A small, rushing object shot ahead."

ning motor, and the next instant a small, rushing object shot around a bend ahead, and, in two great wings of flying water came tearing down at us.

"The *Paris à la mer Race*!" said Pomeroy.

We knew of this race but had forgotten it. Giving the *Beaver* a sheer toward the bank we slowed our speed to make as little wash as possible for the

6

small flyer, which shot past close aboard, her two occupants waving to us. Close on her heels came another, then two more almost abreast. A few minutes later we passed one of the little gliding boats, and although we slowed down she looked as if she were " hitting only the high places " when she met the *Beaver's* swell; in fact, her crew of two appeared to have all that they could do to hang on as she squattered from one wave to the next. For an hour or two we were kept busy dodging the racers; then came a stream of cripples, and one of my companions said, unkindly:

" That's your class, Dan, you brute ! " But that sort of talk was good for Dan; it made him ambitious.

Several yachts and small steamers were following up the race, and their passengers looked curiously at our American ensign. The farther inland we got the more curiosity this and the *Beaver* herself excited, her seagoing type being so entirely different from that of the long, slim, shallow, lightly built power boats of inland waters with their square cabin houses and dainty lace curtains screening the large, plate-glass windows. We were sometimes asked why we had such small, round windows in the cabin, and why the latter was built so low.

It was impossible for these inlanders, many of whom had never seen the sea, to picture in their minds a wave which would sweep clean over the boat's high bows.

We had hoped to get into Rouen early in the afternoon, but the tide turned a little above Caude-bec, and we made poor progress. The motor also appeared to be running badly, working so heavily that it led me to think the propeller might be fouled. At the same time the resoldered fuel pipe began to leak again, and finally, as we were making such poor progress, we decided to stop the motor, drop our kedge anchor, and give things an overhauling. I went overboard, and on examining the propeller discovered a twisted rope of grass wound so tightly around the boss, and jammed in between the boss and tail shaft, that I was unable to budge it with my hands alone and had to get a sharp knife to saw it through. No wonder Dan had been working overtime! But when Dan really chose to work it took more than a bale of hay to stop him!

We served the fuel pipe with some surgeon's plaster reënforced with copper wire and then, as the tide was running out so fast that we saw no hope of reaching Rouen before dark, decided to wait for the flood and save fuel. By this time we were well above the influence of the *mascaret*, but even as high as Rouen the flood tide arrives at a few centimeters higher level than the water it meets, which on encountering it turns immediately and runs the other way. There is no " slack water " interval.

Taking the young flood we started up the river. The darkness came presently, but Rouen is a port of entry for big steamers, and although the river is tortuous the channel is fairly wide and well lighted. Laying our courses from light to light we made good time, reaching Rouen at about midnight. As the *Beaver* belonged to the Touring Club of France, we hunted up the club's landing and tied up there for the night.

The following morning we were met by some ladies, members of Mr. Pomeroy's family, and a friend who had come down to join us for the trip up to Paris. Wishing to readjust the fuel pump and make a few other necessary adjustments about the motor, I remained in my *mécanicien* clothes and, being still at work, was unable to go up to the hotel for *déjeuner*. Presently a waiter came down to the boat, bringing me a bottle of wine and some sandwiches which the others had sent me; then he

70

Rouen.

hung about asking silly questions until, being a bit
warm from my efforts, I frightened him away. Before long a bystander kindly informed me that my
patron was coming, and after a delay in taking fuel
we started up the river. Pomeroy presently tired
of being a swell, and so in time did Ranney. Both
retired to the cabin to reappear presently as members of the *équipage,* much to the delight of the
ladies, one of whom, being accustomed to driving
an automobile, very quickly acquired complete mastery of the *Beaver,* even to the going in and out of
locks and bringing the boat gently alongside. So
the unusual spectacle presented to the astonished

river population was that of a large seagoing motor boat flying the American flag, piloted by a young lady, and manned by two rather stylish and one very disreputable *mécaniciens*. Pomeroy, presenting the ship's papers and interviewing the lock keepers, was regarded as commandant; Ranney, in a very pretty guernsey, a crimson neckerchief, and new suit of blue dungarees which he had brought to an æsthetic shade of color pleasing to his eye by repeated soakings and wringing out, handled the stern warp as gracefully as might the chorus of " Pinafore," occasionally reprimanding Pomeroy or myself for some thoughtless negligence on our part. The two were very much admired; they were so pretty. But for me, stoker and *matelot quelconque,* in a blue flannel shirt and a pair of nameless nether garments, there was no admiration at all; only awe for the terrors of my calling. When the blast lamps began to roar into the hoods of the ignition chambers a flutter passed through the crowd, and the timid ones withdrew from proximity; but when I cranked Dan and he started off with the roar of a racing car there would be a sudden rear march. I soon learned how to fire salutes out of the stern exhaust at will. This could be done by releasing the clutch, throwing the throttle wide and closing

"The Seine from Rouen to Maisons Lafitte is charmingly picturesque."

it sharply again. The result was that the over-charge hung fire until well along the exhaust and then fired out astern with the report of a four-inch gun. The effect upon the population was very interesting: those near by ran from, and those at a

73

distance toward the boat, so that there were two streams of traffic moving rapidly in opposite directions.

We were three days in going up to Paris. Dan was on his good behavior, but the river was so charming that we took it by easy stages, stopping for lunch in some picturesque little hamlet where we were served with delicious omelets and *poulet roti* and salad, in a fresh little bower under trel-. lises covered with ivy or grape. Knowing all of the more attractive places along the river, we would arrange our day's run as in automobiling, so as to stop for the night at some quaint, interesting place where there was a good hotel; no difficult task in France.

The Seine from Rouen to Maisons Lafitte is charmingly picturesque; there is no perceptible current as the river is " canalized." The locks are far apart and one passes through them very quickly, there being special locks for yachts and small vessels. The Seine itself winds in a serpentine course through a lovely, undulating country which is park-like in its picturesque order and freedom from inartistic elements, such as factories or squalid towns and villages. There are model farms with well-kept fields, stretches of forest here and there,

stately châteaux, thrusting their Gothic towers
above the treetops, and beautifully kept estates
sloping down to the river, with charming villas
tucked away and seen in swift vistas through the
intervening green. Sometimes the walls and ruined
towers of some fortress rise gauntly from the summit of a hill commanding the surrounding coun-

Mantes, as we came up the river.

try; at Les Andelys one enjoys from the river the
most imposing view to be had of the ruins of
Château Gaillard, which was built in a single year
by Richard Cœur de Lion.

At Vernon we discovered the wire cable of our
steering gear to be so badly chafed as to make it
dangerous, and as both tiller lines had been renewed
since leaving London, it was evident that wire cable
would not be practicable for the purpose. That

75

which we had was the same used for automobile hand brakes, but it was obliged to pass through too many leads before reaching the steering wheel. It seemed to me that ratline stuff would be much better, as the strain of steering was comparatively slight, the difficulty with the wire being the constant bending and straightening, but as we were unable to get ratline stuff I spliced a piece of manila into the wire to take us to Paris.

On arriving at Paris, or more properly Puteaux, we lay at the float of the Isle de Puteaux Tennis and Rowing Club, of which Ranney was a member.

Here, although Dan was by this time working soberly and conscientiously, we judged it wise to have him thoroughly overhauled by an expert, and as Linton Hope and Company, our builders, had given us credit on the Paris agents of the motor, we had expert advice and treatment. Three days later, tuned to the fighting pitch and having thoroughly found himself, Dan was ready for his long climb over the hills of eastern France and down again into the valley of the Rhine.

CHAPTER V

N the first day of August, just six weeks behind our schedule as planned, we sailed from Puteaux and proceeded up the river, having with us for the run up through the city of Paris two of Mr. Pomeroy's family and the expert adjuster, who, as a matter of fact, had found practically nothing to do to the motor. At the Suresnes lock the keeper told us that the Paris-St. Germain passenger steamer *La Touriste* was due, and asked us to wait a few minutes as the steamer had the right of way. Dan always hated waiting, and I, as engineer, hated to have him do so; if I stopped him it was necessary to start the lamps, and if I turned him over slowly he would cool down sufficiently to lose all interest in his work, and would usually start off again firing unevenly. In the locks we usually left the clutch in and let him tug away at the stern warp, but in the present instance, as there was no good place conveniently at hand to tie up

77

to, we kept under way, maneuvering about, going ahead and astern and marking time while waiting for *La Touriste* to lock through.

Unfortunately, we had been unable to get the proper stuff for our steering lines in Paris, and as the splice which I had put in at Vernon appeared to be in good condition and the wire, though slightly frayed out where it ran through the leads, still serviceable, I had not put in a new line. Just as *La Touriste* was about to come out of the lock, somebody aboard the *Beaver* dropped one of our fenders overboard. As we were moving ahead at the time it had slipped astern before anybody could grab up the hook and catch it, so in order to secure it as quickly as possible and slip into the lock before some of the other boats which were waiting should preëmpt our berth, I reversed quickly and backed down on the fender. With good sternway the *Beaver* would steer very nicely, but the strain of water on the rudder as the sternway increased proved too much for the chafed wire cable tiller line which parted just above the spot where I had spliced the rope into it. The next instant the rope itself, which was fast at its forward end to the chain which ran over the sprocket of the steering wheel, dropped down into the shaft pit and like a flash was whipped around the rapidly revolving shaft. The sudden strain snapped the wire cable on the port side, the heavy chain followed the rope and was partly wound around the shaft, while the free end was whipping around beneath the wheel

At the clubhouse landing, Isle de Puteaux.

and threatening to amputate the foot of anyone within reach.

Of course, the wheel was useless, and I did not know what would happen if the chain should jam, but we were charging astern and under the bows of *La Touriste*, which was coming rapidly out of the lock, so that I did not dare throw out the clutch until I had turned the propeller wheel ahead, checked the boat's way and got her in a position of safety. Then I stopped the motor, and we managed to disentangle the chain and get into the lock, steering by the tiller.

It was very annoying to be compelled to go up through the city of Paris in man-o'-war launch fashion, one hand steering from the stern while another ran the engine, especially as steering a heavy boat like the *Beaver* with a short iron tiller was no lady's pastime, but we were anxious to get to Lagny that evening and it was already early afternoon. So we made the best of it.

At the *octroi* station, just below the Pont du jour, an officer, who from his uniform looked as if he must be at least a rear admiral, signaled us to stop while he came alongside. The current was swift, and there was a boat coming down ahead and another going up astern and the handling of the *Beaver* was awkward owing to the disabled steering gear, but there we had to wait until his Excellency came alongside. I opened Dan up and he roared in a way that made it impossible to hear a word said, but nothing could so convey the impression of frantic impatience as Dan, if properly tormented, and that was the idea which I wanted him to express. The *octroi* man looked at him askance,

80

and while still at a distance began to ask if we had
any chickens or *pré-salé* lamb and I don't know
what. At least, that's what he probably said; no
one could hear what he really said. But everybody
shouted " *Non!* " to *everything* that he said, and
they answered as if they meant it. Then Dan began to make sounds which took all desire to board
us from the man's bewildered mind, and he made
a despairing signal which may have meant for us
to go up the Seine or down somewhere else. We
chose the Seine, and started off with a royal salute
and much churning of water under the stern.

We pushed on upstream, past the Eifel Tower
and the Trocadero and the Louvre and Notre
Dame. At Ivry we landed our *mécanicien* and at
St. Maur left the Seine and, passing through a tunnel six hundred meters in length, came out at Join-
ville le Pont, on the Marne.

At Lagny we partook of a farewell dinner with
our guests who bade us " bon voyage " and returned to Paris by rail, and we went back aboard
the boat in a sad and thoughtful frame of mind,
to meditate upon the big Continent which must be
traversed before the *Beaver's* nose should be turned
toward home again.

From Lagny, which is only about twenty kilometers from Paris, our course lay across France in an easterly direction to the German frontier, thence through Alsace-Lorraine to Strassburg, where we were to enter the Rhine.

Up to this point we had been in fairly open water, the Thames, the English Channel, the Seine; all navigable for seagoing vessels, but at Lagny the "mud-holing" began which was to continue for about three hundred and fifty miles until we struck the Rhine.

Looking back upon this part of our voyage we feel extremely glad to have experienced it, but I do not think that any of us would care to attempt anything of the sort again. As far as actual progress is concerned, one may form an idea of the tediousness of this variety of travel by a glance at the schedule of our itinerary on page 84, which explains itself.

Some years ago I took a thirty-foot boat from Greenwich, Conn., to the Dismal Swamp, Virginia, by the inside passage. After this trip I thought that I had seen something of canals and locks, although as I recall it there were only about sixty or seventy miles of the former and about a dozen or so of the latter. Compare this with the two hundred and five locks between Paris and

"Through stately avenues of grand old trees."

ACROSS EUROPE IN A MOTOR BOAT

Day's runs of the Beaver from Paris to Strassburg,
via the Marne River and the Marne-au-Rhin Canal.

DATE	From	To	Kilometers	Locks
Aug. 1	Paris (Puteaux)	Lagny	50	3
2	Lagny	Charly	85	8
3	Charly	Epernay	68	8
4	Epernay	Ablancourt	48	9
5	Ablancourt	Contrisson	40	16
6	Contrisson	Longeville	23	24
7	Longeville	Naix les Forges	19	19
8	Naix les Forges	Mauvages	22	14
9	Mauvages	Foug	30	14
10	Foug	Toul	9	11
11	Toul	Nancy	33	5
12	Nancy	Parroy	38	11
13	Parroy	St. Blasien	18	9
14	St. Blasien	Arzweiler	34	11
15	Arzweiler	Hochfelden	34	32
16	Hochfelden	Strassburg	25	11

Total, 16 days from PARIS to STRASSBURG. 576 kil. (360 miles) 205 locks.

Strassburg and figure also on tunnels, bridges, and so thick a stream of traffic that we would often find five or six canal boats waiting to lock through, and one will understand the objection to this form of travel if one is in a hurry. Between Paris and Strassburg the locks are single, and the boats are built to fit them as a boottree fits a boot, with the

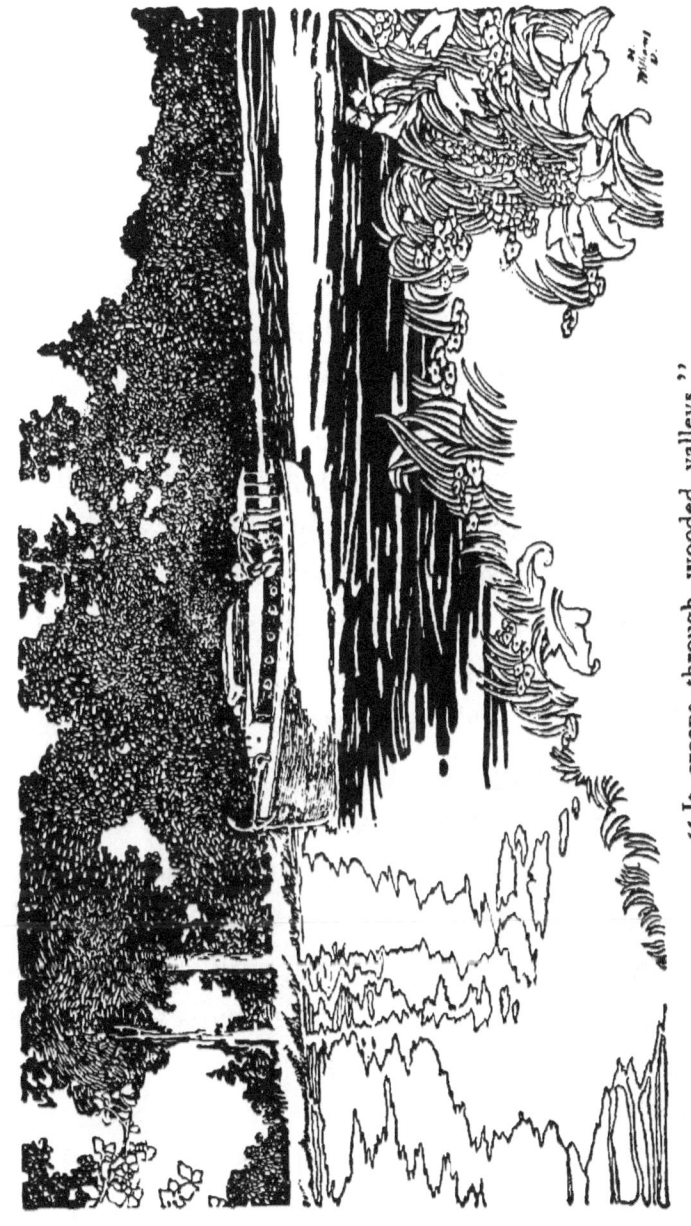

"It creeps through wooded valleys."

result that it may take fifteen or twenty minutes to lock a boat through. Thanks to the canal authorities we had the power of *trématage,* or right of way, otherwise we might never have got out of that canal!

But no words can describe the picturesque and ever-changing beauty of the entire route! No road nor bypath which we had ever seen in France could compare with the intimate charm of this winding water way. It creeps through wooded valleys, skirts the edges of wild, bracken-covered hills where one may look for miles across the intervening country and see the mountains, blue with distance. At times the canal will lead for the entire day through stately avenues of grand old trees whose interlacing foliage screens the heat of the midsummer sun. Often, from some high slope one may look down into a verdant valley where a broad river winds away through forest-covered hills with here and there the Gothic towers of a stately château or the ruined ones of some mediæval fortress thrust up above the luscious foliage. There are such views to be had and others more pastoral of the valleys of the Marne and the Meuse and the Moselle. The two latter are crossed by the canal on high stone bridges similar to those built for a railroad. Also, there are tunnels where the canal bores through the heart of hill and mountain. The longest of these is at Mauvages, the crest of the divide between the valleys of the Marne and the Moselle, and is five kilometers in length.

The canal water is fresh and clean and limpid, spring-fed from the banks, receiving tributary streams, and high up in the Vosges it is reënforced from a pumping station, as the traffic is heavy and a lockful of water is lost with every passing boat. The descent of this water creates a current throughout and keeps the canal free of scum and *débris*.

Most interesting of all are the quaint experiences which come to one during this sort of a journey. In our *mécanicien* costumes of blue dungaree we were invariably accepted as three professionals engaged to transport the boat to the Rhine for some *richard Américain*. As the result, we were received by the canal folk upon terms of friendly equality, and many a long and interesting chat we had with them. There are very distinct social grades among those who follow the canals as a profession; a society which ranges all the way from the patron of the beautiful and stately *péniche* or full-sized barge to the poor and humble *équipage* of the dingy, dirty little *montluçon*, a scow somewhat resembling a Filipino casco and of which the motive power is a team composed of a bedraggled under-fed donkey and the bedraggled, under-fed wife of the patron, hitched tandem, the donkey leading, while the lord and master lounges across the tiller and smokes his pipe. This sort of an outfit is regarded like the pariah of the East. The whole family lives in a little shack in the stern of the scow. There are very few of this sort.

But the household of the handsome *péniche* is a very different matter. In America, whether rightly or wrongly, canal folk are regarded as rather rough citizens; in France their respectability is unquestioned, and their social caste appears to be that of the prosperous farmer. We found them invariably kind, courteous, intelligent, and self-respecting. The little cottages on their big boats were models of cleanliness and comfort, always freshly painted, with lace curtains in the windows and usually having flower boxes and plants on the little piazzas. The wives were strong, wholesome-looking women who could steer the boat into a lock or catch a turn with a wire hawser and then go back to the oven again. The children seemed very well cared for.

At the quaint little inns along the bank which

cater to these people, and where we have eaten
many a good dinner, we often found a group of
these canal *mariniers* playing dominoes or billiards
or sipping absinthe with their friends, but never

A fair *éclusière*.

once did we see any roughness of conduct or hear
any bad talk. Sometimes in the day's work we
would do them a good turn, giving a man a lift to
his boat a few kilometers farther on or perhaps
putting the *Beaver's* nose against a barge and shov-
ing it into position, and often they did us one, let-

ting us tie up alongside for the night and using their boat as a landing stage.

After leaving Lagny we pushed on up the Marne against a current of perhaps three miles an hour, varying with the character of the stream. The Marne water is beautifully clear; one could see the bottom everywhere. It is also full of fish and appears to remain so with very little restocking despite the fact that there are fishing parties every hundred feet in the vicinity of the villages, and I do not think that we were ever on any part of the river where there were not several anglers in sight. Fishing is without doubt the national sport of France. Never in any part of the world have I seen such perseverance or enthusiasm shown for angling by all classes of society. One has only to walk along the banks of the Seine in Paris to appreciate this; rain or shine, winter or summer, in scorching heat or driving snow, there is always a battalion of the much-respected army of anglers. In Paris they are a pathetic guild because they scarcely ever catch anything, and when they do it is not more than three inches long, and being whipped up at the end of a long bamboo pole has usually to be plucked out of the top branches of a tree.

"The intimate charm of this water way."

But anywhere along the river let a really good-sized fish be caught, and the day's work is over. The *pêcheur* cannot wait a minute to exhibit his catch. Wrapping the prize carefully in a sheet torn from *Le Matin*, on which he has been sitting, he places it in his inside pocket, carefully buttons his coat and departs hotfoot for the nearest *café*. There, no matter whether he is known or not, the fish is put on exhibition, and the whole story of the capture is related to the accompaniment of many *ma fois* and *sapristis* from the interesting and admiring audience.

Pomeroy was returning to the boat one day when a young girl, stammering with excitement, rushed up to him and cried:

" O M'sieu, will you have the kindness to assist at the capture of a very large fish ? "

Pomeroy hastened toward the river while the girl sped on after further reënforcements. Down on the bank was a *pêcheur*, capering up and down and yelling. His pole was bent double, and out in the stream the line was cutting the water in big circles, but although fully equipped with all that was needed to land the fish he was so excited that he could only prance up and down and howl. By the time his fellow-townsfolk had arrived the fish was about done for, and the fisherman, realizing the fact that he had arrived at a crisis in his life, pulled himself together and managed to land a good-sized pike.

At Charly I viewed the scene of a disaster which had befallen me in March. Ranney and I had taken Pomeroy's canvas canoe up to Epernay by rail and thence paddled back to Paris, a five days' trip. The river was high and very swift in places, and at Charly lock I tried to run the rapids. Ranney, not caring for the temperature of the water, got out on the bank with the camera to get some views of my last moments. He nearly succeeded, as a back eddy whipped the canoe almost under the fall, but getting clear by hard paddling I had shot well through the rapids when for some reason which I never quite understood I got spilled out. It was very fresh in the water, and after swimming to the bank with the canoe I saw Ranney's hat spinning off downstream and had to swim after that.

CHAPTER VI

HAT night we spent at Charly, and in the morning on starting had a little more trouble with Dan. Altogether, this was a vexing day. I have before me Pomeroy's log book, battered and semipulpified from a soaking in the Black Sea. Under the printed headings of "Courses," "Winds," "Sea Swell," "Barometer," and so on, I find the following which I am tempted to quote verbatim, although conscious that to publish any part of this record is a breach of trust which risks a valued friendship.

"August 3d. Warm and cloudy. Repacked head of fore cylinder. Started. Fore engine missing. Forgot coat (Hank's) on dock. Returned. Cleared quicker. O. K. Hit blades of screw in Damery lock. Abe whitens his shoes and Hank still without soap. Hank finds his shoes in his own locker with typewriter. Walked over to Epernay, two kilometers, and dined at Hôtel de l'Europe.

94

Slept well after walk back under stars carrying our lunch for to-morrow, mostly wine. Had a strong current against us all day in the Marne."

Under " Remarks " it says:

" 3.05, cleared Vandière lock. Going in fair— lead of tiller line carried away and we put her nose into the bank."

I trust that nobody will be so mean as to try to trace any connection between the above entries and the fact that they all happened at Epernay, which is the center of the champagne country! Hitting the propeller blades was my work. Damery lock had sloping walls pitched in at an angle of forty-five degrees. In starting the motor to go out, the stern swung too far in and wiped the rims of the blades, scoring them badly. I did not get over this for several days when I did it again! Long before we reached the Black Sea, however, this had become of so frequent occurrence as no longer to arouse any emotion.

Let no one imagine that this canal navigation is a pastime adapted to children and invalids. Where the traffic is as heavy as on the Marne-au-Rhin Canal it would be very easy to lose your boat. One is constantly dodging in and out between big, heavily loaded barges carrying stone and coal and wine and railroad iron, the mere drift of which as they come together would flatten a boat like the *Beaver* should she happen to get nipped between. There are many dangers of this sort. There are the big " empties " to avoid, as being light and drawing only six or eight inches they travel fast, are impossible to steer, and in a stiff breeze take up the whole canal. There is the danger of parting a line from the rush of water when the lock is filling, and being dashed against the sides or end, and there is a danger which sounds absurd but is quite actual; that is in miscalculating the relative time taken for a swinging bridge to open toward you and that of your approach. Then there is the constant danger to the screw from the inward slant of the stone facing of the canal bank.

Altogether the work needs constant vigilance and something of the qualities of a chauffeur, especially when racing past a long line of boats to get into a lock with another line coming from the opposite direction. One may ask: " But why take such chances? " The answer is: " Because if you do not you are apt to get frozen in when the winter comes."

In the extract from Pomeroy's log book the accident to the steering gear is mentioned. On this occasion it was amusing; that is, to Pomeroy and myself. We were at the time " standing off and on " in a little canal " port," waiting to go into a lock. This " port " or basin was perhaps fifty meters in diameter, the lock opening directly into it. Pomeroy and I were sitting up forward admiring the evolutions of Ranney, who was having his hands full to keep the boat in position against the rush of the water coming down as the lock was emptied. He was not asking any help, thank you, but he was very much occupied, as we could tell from the row Dan was raising and the thrash of the propeller as he forged ahead or went astern. At this time he had not handled the boat a great deal in restricted waters, and presently Pomeroy said:

" Perhaps you had better take her."

" No," said I. " The propeller blades are enough damage to my account for one day. Let him alone. He is doing well and learning fast. Don't say a word. If he biffs the lock, pretend that you do not notice it, and try to pretend it better than you did when I hit the blades ! "

We sat quite still. As the last of the water came out and the gates began to open, the current swung the boat's head off to port. Ranney put his helm

97

astarboard and backed out, a very proper maneuver. He got well clear of the bank, and then to
swing the bow sharply back into the right position
for entering he went " full ahead," at the same
time porting his helm.

The theory was correct, but the bow failed to
swing. To Pomeroy and me it looked as if Ranney was tired of waiting for the lock to open and
had decided to get a good start and go across lots.

" We're going to hit! " said Pomeroy.

" Don't say a word," said I. " Don't even look
around; just keep on talking as if nothing had happened."

The *Beaver* charged into the bank and started
to climb up. We did not move, but kept on talking as if unconscious of anything unusual. No
sound from Ranney, who was expectantly waiting
some comment. Presently we glanced about indif-
ferently, and there stood Ranney with an expression of the most impatient pugnacity. We looked
away.

" I suppose you think that I'm a d—— fool? "
he asked, in an injured tone.

" Not at all. Why do you ask? "

Ranney looked disgusted. " Well," he growled,
" when I put the wheel over your blooming steer-

ing gear busted, and before I could find out what was the matter, she bumped! "

Day after day we climbed tediously up the long flight of stairs leading to the highlands between Meuse and Meurthe-et-Moselle. At Chalons-sur-Marne we skirted the Catalaunian Fields, where in 451 B.C. the great army of the Huns was defeated by the Romans and their allies the Franks and Visigoths.

Sometimes the canal became so choked with traffic that it did not seem to us as if we should ever get out into open water again. Glancing at the table on page 84, one sees a day when we made but nine kilometers and passed through only eleven locks! Another day shows thirty-four kilometers and thirty-two locks, all depending on the traffic and the duration of the " waits." If we had not been a month behind our schedule and could have possessed our souls in peace it would not have been so bad, but with visions of the water in the river Maine dropping day by day, and also of arriving at Sulina and embarking upon the Black Sea, so named for its evil reputation, after the change of seasons, these delays were simply maddening. Pomeroy alone accepted the situation placidly, as is evidenced by this naïve extract from his log:

8   99

"Wednesday, August 7th.—Morning fair but cloudy. At lock twenty-nine filled our water cask from a spring by lock—kind old lady lent us a bucket. On leaving she presented us with a nosegay from her garden, simple, old-fashioned flowers. Hank will never get any soap I'm sure. Tie up at No. 15 at the wood wharf. Abe has his clothes washed. Lock keeper's two daughters very pretty. Mother fat, but a sweet smile.   Very cold toward morning."

We crossed the valley of the Meuse on a high canal bridge, and it was rather an odd sensation to look from the deck of one's boat into the river beneath. At last, upon the eighth day "outward," or to be more accurate, "inward bound" from Paris, we found ourselves at the top of the divide between the Marne and the Moselle one thousand feet above sea level. Here is another extract from the log:

"Thursday, August 8th.—Beautiful morning, clear and cold. Mist over water. Numbers of boats bound east all through the night, hurrying to get to the tunnel (La Voute) of Mauvages in time to go through at seven. Passed five east-bound boats between 14 and 15. This very green valley of the Ormain gets more beautiful as we go up. The canal is on the side of the hill, and the river bottom is always below us. Hank's famous grass hitch is often used. Hank still on the soap borrow and Abe diligent with his white shoes—has two pairs and works 'em watch and watch. After getting permission to go through tunnel under our own power took *Beaver* to entrance of tunnel and walked back to No. 1 for dinner."

The " famous grass hitch " consisted of taking a handful of the long tough marsh grass which fringed the bank and catching a clove hitch with it around one of the awning stanchions, thereby obviating the necessity of taking a line ashore when compelled to tie up and wait.

At Mauvages we were confronted by a tunnel through the mountain, five kilometers long (over three miles) and unlighted. There is a chain boat which tows the waiting barges through, making a daily passage in either direction. The speed of this train is about a kilometer an hour! We had been told that we should have to tow through behind this line as boats were not permitted to go through under their own power for fear of the fumes which they left in the tunnel. On some former occasion it appears that a small steamer left fumes which caused the asphyxiation and death of two persons on the towing flotilla.

Spending nearly five hours in such a black, depressing hole was such a cheerless prospect that Pomeroy hunted up the superintendent, and by the charm of his personality and his insidious blandishments obtained permission for us to go through alone that night after the arrival of the tow from the other side. We were instructed to go to the mouth of the tunnel and to wait there until the tow emerged, then to proceed through, slowly and carefully, taking great care not to leave any fumes in transit. Accordingly, we got under way, and proceeding through a deep, winding defile between steep, rugged hills, came presently to where the black mouth of the tunnel opened before us like the entrance of the Styx in its course to the Infernal Regions. Here we moored to the stone facing of the canal and waited.

This place is weirdly striking; a deep amphitheater between precipitous, fern-covered slopes which higher up are wooded with beech and chestnut. A curve in the canal closes the entrance, while at the other end the black arch of the tunnel is built in a great wall of solid masonry. On either side of this wall a stone stairway ascends to a terrace above the arch, and from the center of this another long stairway leads straight up the hillside and disappears in the dense foliage above. The floor of the big amphitheater is the black water of the

"The black mouth of the tunnel opened before us like the entrance of the Styx."

canal. Although midsummer and still early in the afternoon, the light was deeply subdued, and a cold, damp draught of air reeking of mold fanned faintly from the tunnel's mouth. Beautiful as the place was in an eerie way, it was at the same time depressing from its sad loneliness and absence of all sign of human habitation.

The moment that we stopped the motor a chorus of wild, discordant sounds came welling out from the heart of the mountain; deep, rumbling groans, undertoning a diapason of clamoring human voices which sounded like the distant shrieking of the souls of the damned. They died away, then arose again in a confused medley which was accompanied by the mournful clanking of chains.

"I thought that this place looked like the gates of hell," said somebody, "and now there is no longer any doubt of it. Listen to that infernal row!"

The noises seemed to swell out in fresh waves of sound with the faint draughts of air wafted from the tunnel. We decided that they must come from the chain boat and its long train of barges, for although the line must still have been over a mile deep in the mountain, the tunnel itself was a great speaking tube and capable of transmitting sound for an indefinite distance. When we stood at the mouth of the tunnel the noises became louder and more defined; we could distinctly hear the clanking of the chain cable as it was reeled in over the drum of the towboat, and the human voices were a combination of song, conversation, and occasional yells from the *mariniers*, who were perhaps amusing themselves after the manner of small boys in the tunnel under a causeway.

As the day waned the place became more and more grewsome. Heavy shadows hung in the ravine, while overhead the sky was still brightly blue. The sounds from the tunnel grew gradually louder and more discordant. Deep in the gloom lights began to spark and the individual voices became intelligible. Finally, when within a few meters of the mouth of the tunnel some *marinier* struck up a song; others joined the chorus, which sounded like a chant, or pæon of praise and thankfulness at getting the weight of the mountain off their backs, and so singing to the accompaniment of the clanking chain, they crawled out into the fading daylight.

As it was then after six o'clock we decided to dine before going through, and therefore walked back to a little *auberge* in the village, where they gave us a very good *compot* of hare, *haricots verts*, an omelet of bread and cheese, with the wine of the country, a *petit vin gris*, which is a pink, effervescent wine, and tastes like sour champagne.

It was about nine o'clock when we got back to

the boat, having to walk some distance. Getting
Dan well heated up we ran him until both cylinders
were firing completely, so as to leave no fumes in
our wake; then placing two lanterns forward to
throw a glare against the walls on either side, we
started in. It was our intention to proceed slowly
and carefully, but as I do not care much for tunnels, and happened to be steering, I presently
turned Dan loose and let him go full speed. In
spite of her smoke and gas condensers the towboat
had left fumes enough in the place to make us
cough, and the air was cold and heavy. Steering
the boat was also nervous work; there was nothing
to head for but a vague, central zone of murk, and
the pale glare of the lanterns on the sides of the
wall had a peculiar hypnotizing effect on the eyes,
making it difficult to focus, while the friction of
the water between the boat and the tunnel's sides
dragged with an alternating pull, first on one side,
then on the other, according to which wall the boat
was nearer, making it hard to steer a true course.
About halfway through we got an icy shower from
a spring which had burst through the roof; apparently this spot was undergoing repair, as we had
observed a scaffolding on a barge near the entrance.

But the most nerve-racking thing of all was the

indescribable din made by our motor and thrown down in terrific reverberations from the walls. Dan was always a noisy beast, but in that tunnel his clamor was a thing to burst the tympani and tear the nerves out by the roots. I have been through five naval engagements and a Strauss concert, but that racket in the tunnel could have given cards and spades to a duet between a boiler factory and a rapid-fire gun, and made a Strauss concert sound like whispered words of love!

None of us received any sense of the lapse of time while in the tunnel; it might have been five minutes or fifty, and when suddenly the glimmer of light disappeared from the walls it gave us a dreadful shock. The night was dark, and the lanterns forward so blinded the vision of everything ahead that the impression received as we suddenly emerged from the tunnel was that of charging against a solid black wall. Indeed, I was on the point of reversing hard when the feeling of the air told me that we had come out.

From this point we began the descent of the long slope down into the valley of the Moselle. The feature of this part of the voyage most impressed upon my memory is that of getting overboard in the cold water three or four times a day to clear the grass from the screw. There was also some beautiful scenery.

Not far beyond the Mauvages tunnel we arrived at another one which is two kilometers long. Here there were two-hour intervals through the day for boats coming and going, and as the tunnel was too narrow to permit of our turning or even of squeezing past a boat coming from the opposite direction, it behooved us to go through at the right time. There were some boats waiting at the mouth, bound in the same direction as ourselves, and the captain of one of these told us that if we hurried we could get through before the time was up. As it meant a delay of two hours to wait, we decided to take a chance, and accordingly entered. The other end was barely visible as a pin prick of light, and when we were about halfway through we discovered that there were moving objects between it and ourselves. Pomeroy got his glass on them, and announced in some excitement that it was a barge coming in our direction, as he could see the horses out ahead.

The situation promised to be very awkward, as we could not steer the *Beaver* backward in such narrow quarters. It looked to me as if the boat were going in the same direction as ourselves; even

Where the canal enters the moat of the city wall at Toul.

if she were not, the best way seemed to be to hold on our course and bully *them* into backing out, as they were just inside the entrance. As I was running the boat at the time I held on ahead in spite of the impassioned protests of Pomeroy, who finally, convinced that through sheer, pig-headed obstinacy I was getting deeper and deeper into the mess, grabbed the reversing wheel and stopped us. Much pained at this breach of etiquette, I dropped the wheel and lit a cigarette. Dan was filling the place with his deafening uproar, and, not satisfied with the general demoralization, began to miss one cylinder. It was dark as pitch, our feeble lantern accentuating the gloom. Pomeroy was trying to make me hear his argument against the roars of Dan; Ranney was quite indifferent as to what happened, and I was sitting in the corner of the cockpit pouting. Far ahead we could see the legs of the animals twinkling against the tiny arc of light. Suddenly the humor of the thing struck me and cheered me up.

" I will get out and go on ahead," I shouted in Pomeroy's ear, " and see which way they are going. If you see me wave, come ahead."

So I got on the towpath and trotted down through the mud for half a mile to the end of the tunnel, and there found two barges going out. Their crews were staring astern with their eyes sticking out of their heads, and I did not blame them, considering the unholy noises proceeding from the black depths beyond!

"At Toul we crossed the Moselle on a big stone bridge."

At Toul we crossed the Moselle on a big stone bridge with high arches. We did not stop to see the old cathedral of St. Etienne, famous for its thirteenth-century cloister. There was also another tunnel, described in the guide book as an

" *ouvrage d'art fort curieux*," being five hundred meters long. It did not impress us. Toul is very heavily garrisoned, and in one place the canal leads into and along the moat of the city for a considerable distance. All of the surrounding hills are strongly fortified.

Nancy was our next " port of call," and there we spent a day, as this city is interesting and beautiful. It was the ancient capital of Lorraine, and the Place Stanislaus in the center of the town is exceedingly striking. Formerly Nancy was famous as the seat of the dukes of Lorraine. To-day it is famous for embroideries and macaroons.

CHAPTER VII

FTER leaving Nancy the canal wanders off and loses itself in a pretty, pastoral country remote from everything. We fetched up for the night at a place called Parroy, a quaint little village high up on a hill surrounded by meadows which were covered with cows. The following morning on awakening I found that Pomeroy had been suffering all night from an acute intestinal indigestion, and after abusing him for not having called me I attempted to give him some medicine, but being half asleep and my fingers stiff and swollen from daily burns and bruises, I cleverly managed to drop the bottle on the fly wheel, where it broke and went to join the interesting mixture in the bilge. Pomeroy was feeling too bad to say anything, so I said it for him.

" Anyway," said I, " you must have a milk diet, so I will go up to the village and get some milk, and some more of this stuff at the same time."

" You may succeed in getting the dope," said he, " but you will not get any milk."

" Why not? There is nothing here but cows."

" Just the same," said he, " you will not get any milk. I have lived twenty years in France."

Not wishing to argue with a sick man I got dressed and departed. At the top of the hill I found the villagers in a state of wild excitement. A woman told me that a mad dog (*chien enragé*) had bitten a boy. Everybody was talking at once, and arguing over the proper course of treatment. I told them to take the boy at once to Nancy, where there was, or ought to be, a Pasteur dispensary, which they promised to do. Then I asked if they had killed the dog, meaning to instruct them to send the corpse along with the boy for the purpose of diagnosis, but they told me that the dog was still at large.

" Then shoot him at once."

" That cannot be done, m'sieu', because the owner is in Paris."

" Is it, then, that you do not like the owner, and want him to return and be bitten also? "

" But non, m'sieu', only one does not shoot a dog without the consent of the owner."

" Then," said I, " he will no doubt bite some

more boys and the other dogs and perhaps a few cows or a goat, and they will all go mad and run around biting! "

"The canal wanders off and loses itself in a pretty pastoral country."

But they appeared to regard this fearful development as in the hands of the *bon Dieu*!

A woman who told me that she was the mother of eleven living children and some dead ones, the last of whom was malformed, kindly gave me some of the desired drug from her own supply. But when I asked for milk she shook her head.

"You will not be able to get any milk, m'sieu'," she said, with decision.

"But why not? There are a great many cows and also some calves. Where this occurs I have always found that there is milk."

"There is milk, m'sieu', but it has all gone to the creamery."

"Nevertheless, I must have some milk. My friend is at the point of death. Is it not possible to milk one of these cows?"

She looked aghast. "At seven of the morning, m'sieu'! One does not milk a cow as late as that!"

"It has to be done," said I, "if I have to do it myself!"

She shook her head and explained it to some of the neighbors, and they all shook their heads. Eventually some one referred me to a neighbor who was supposed to have a cow without a time lock on the milk locker. When I had stated the urgency of the case this good woman detailed a very pretty and amiable young girl of about twenty to go and coax a little milk from the outraged bovine. I went along with her, to carry the pail. Every cloud has its silver lining. The bitten boy got Pasteurized and Pomeroy got his milk, but that night I dreamed that the whole countryside was full of cows who had gone mad because they could

"At noon of that day we arrived at the German frontier."

not be milked, and were running around biting the pretty milkmaids.

At noon of that day we arrived at the German frontier. In the morning as we were going through a lock the little daughter of the keeper asked us if she and her sister might go with us as far as their school, which was three or four kilometers down the canal. The permission was of course given them, and the two children were greatly delighted with their experience. Although living on the border of France and Lorraine they did not speak a word of French. Later that day a man told me that it was against the law to teach French in the schools of Alsace-Lorraine. I was surprised to hear that this old decision was still enforced; if it is indeed true, it certainly seems a very tyrannical and unenlightened ruling on the part of so great and progressive a nation as the German Empire.

An impression which one receives in this former French province is that France makes a good deal more fuss over Alsace-Lorraine than Alsace-Lorraine makes over France! The type of the people, their appearance, manners, characteristics are all markedly Teutonic, especially in Alsace, and, indeed, there is no reason why they should not be, as this country was German to begin with, before its conquest by the Franks. To-day Lorraine is considered to be French *au fond*; no doubt it is, among the old French aristocracy who claim not to understand the German language and will not receive a Prussian officer socially, but there is no such evidence of loyalty to France among the common people.

At the custom house the German official made a perfunctory visit, asked a few questions about our trip, and dismissed us with his blessing. The following day found us at the summit of the Vosges. We passed through the Neiderweiler tunnel, which is a short one of five hundred meters, and soon afterwards came to the Arzweiler tunnel. Here we learned that two boats had just gone in, and as it would take them two hours to make the passage we decided to wait outside rather than in the tunnel.

In the German canal we had been presented by the canal authorities with a large sign, or " shield " as they called it, which being displayed upon the boat entitled us to the right of way. This " shield " was a plank six feet long by a foot and a half wide and bore the imperative word VORFAHRTS-RECHT in letters which filled the whole plank. It proved of inestimable value as it cleared the way ahead and as soon as it was sighted by the lock keepers they would prepare the lock for us even though about to lock a boat through from the other direction. It sometimes hurt our consciences, I will admit, to take the right of way over some poor devil of a canal-boat captain who had been waiting patiently for hours and who was working for his living while we were amusing ourselves, especially as he was paying his way and we were guests. In fact, we very often waived our privilege on this account.

Passing through the Arzweiler tunnel we came out suddenly on a most beautiful and extraordinary view. We had pierced the summit of the Vosges and below us fell a steep, narrow valley with precipitous slopes heavily wooded on either side. From where we emerged the canal descended in a great, curving flight of watery steps, each lock opening into a basin which in turn opened into the next, forming a water stairway three kilometers in length and containing fifteen steps. The lower ones were half hidden in the foliage and then curved away out of sight in the luscious valley beneath. The whole effect of the place reminded me very much of Japan; the steep, pine-covered hills, the dainty little dwellings with their neat, winding paths and little flights of narrow steps twisting up between the tree trunks, but most of all the bright, clear water shimmering through the fresh foliage precisely as one sees in Japan where a little mountain rivulet will be led successively into a series of

diminutive rice paddies, each terraced against the
hillside and receiving the overflow from the one
above, and so descending to the valley beneath.

" The whole effect of the place reminded me very much of
Japan."

As the locks came so near together we stopped
the motor and " jackassed " the boat down by

hand. Halfway to the bottom we had the only row which befell us during the entire voyage.

A big German barge was coming up light, and we had to pass in one of the basins. The lock keeper wanted us to haul to the sill and tie up, but it looked as if the place he indicated would get us squeezed, so we declined. Apparently the bargee was indifferent as to whether he went to port or starboard or over us, for he gave us no time to haul to either side, starting his team on the run and charging down on the *Beaver* at full speed. Pomeroy was in the boat at the wheel; Ranney was ahead with the towline, and I was on the lock with a check line. The bargee was up forward with his pole, and an elderly lady was at the helm. Seeing the danger, Pomeroy addressed a peremptory remark to her, whereat she put her helm over and bumped head on into the stone wall. This so enraged the captain, a hulking young thickhead, that he directed a stream of violent abuse at Pomeroy, whereupon Pomeroy proceeded to revile him in *Apache* French, Ranney cursed him in German, a splendid tongue for the purpose, and I admonished him in Lime'us Londonese. I have never seen a man give so ferocious an exhibition of rabid rage. He foamed up and down the deck of his

"We lay in the heart of Strassburg."

barge cursing and storming and waving his
clenched fists to heaven, and the more he raved the
more we laughed. Twice he made a motion to
jump out on the lock and devour us, which if carried out might perhaps have earned him something
quieting in the shape of a Yankee " jolt " on the
chin, but he thought better of it. He was like one
of those ferocious dogs which tear up and down
behind the palings of their front fence, snarling
with wild desire to get at you, but quite ignoring
the fact that the front gate is wide open.

We spent the night at Hochfelden, arriving in Strassburg the following day. This interesting city with its wonderful cathedral is too well known for me to attempt to describe. We lay in the heart of the town on the Ill River, off what is known as the Mohren Kopf, and there our American flag excited much interest and curiosity.

We spent three days in Strassburg, refitting, taking stores, and filling up with petroleum, of which we carried about one hundred gallons. Also we had the floors throughout carpeted with linoleum, a great relief to me as it kept Pomeroy from continually scrubbing them. We also laid in medical stores, which are very cheap in Germany; the bulk consisted of quinine, as we had been warned of the malarial fevers of the lower Danube.

On the whole we felt that the most arduous part of our journey lay behind us, while the crucial point, that of getting up the shallow Main and into the old Ludwig Canal, was now removed but a few days. All that we were able to learn on this important question was of the most discouraging character, but as Pomeroy cheerfully remarked, it was simply a case where the *Beaver had* to climb the tree!

In Strassburg we were informed that the law re-

quired us to take a pilot for our run down the
Rhine to the mouth of the river Main. Inasmuch
as we always made it a point to obey the laws of
the country through which we were passing, when
not too inconvenient, we dropped down the Ill
River to the last lock, where we secured the serv-
ices of a thickhead, who claimed to be a licensed
pilot, but whose authenticity we doubted as he had
neither his papers nor that crisp style which char-
acterizes the breed. As there was no one else at
hand we engaged him on the recommendation of
the lock keeper, agreeing to pay him the regular
pilot's fee of thirty marks for the run to Manheim.

Passing through the lock we entered the Little
Rhine, a short sluice from the main stream. Here
our pilot picked up his *ruder bote*, a scow which
towed about as easily as a sea anchor, and we
pushed out into the Rhine.

If you should ever have occasion to navigate
your own boat in European waters do not have
anything to do with a local pilot. He is no good.
On the other hand, the regularly licensed, uni-
formed, gold-laced species with the manners of a
Chesterfield and the style of an admiral will be
found absolutely dependable. In over fifteen hundred miles of dangerous river navigation, although

we only took pilots when required by law for some
short and difficult passage, we had experience with
both kinds. The former is apt to be an ex-deck
hand who knows the banks but not the bottom, or
else a local riverman who has learned where he
can go in his skiff and thinks that he can take you
by the same path. But the duly licensed man is a
wonder. He can take a six-barge tow through a
narrow, tortuous channel where you could toss
your cap on the ledges at either side, and where
the treacherous shoals are shifting from day to day.
Moreover, he can do it at night or through the
early morning river mist more baffling than fog,
and with or against a current which the *Beaver*
could scarcely buck.

Our makeshift pilot needed the whole river to
steer the boat, being apparently unable to get rid
of the idea that he was handling a stone-laden
barge and throwing all of his weight on the wheel,
which could be put over by the pressure of one
finger. Ranney called his attention every few minutes to the danger of parting our tiller lines, but in
spite of that he came near wrecking us some distance down the river. Wishing to sheer into the
bank to drop his *ruder bote*, he twisted the wheel
over so violently as to tear out one of the fair

leads of the steering gear, which jammed and left the boat out of control in the swift current. Fortunately we were standing by; one of us grabbed the wheel while the other jumped after for the tiller, and working together we accomplished our maneuver without mishap.

Said somebody: " The most aggravating thing about this fool is that we don't need him! Why, navigating this river is just like taking a car down the Champs Elysées! "

This is quite true. The Rhine current is fairly swift and with a low river, such as we had, there are a great many shoals, but the courses of the channel are so clearly indicated by range poles from point to point on the bank that there is no excuse for going wrong. At the time the current looked very ferocious to us, but that was before we had navigated the Danube. In the Rhine we could hold our own anywhere if obliged to turn upstream to wait for a ferryboat to cross or a boat bridge to open; later on in the Danube we found many places where we could not stem the current at all. Once or twice on our way down the Rhine, while breasting the current as we waited for a boat bridge to open, I found myself wondering just what would happen if Dan, our motor, were to balk. Our anchor would not have held on that hard, gravelly bottom. Fortunately, however, Dan had overcome the turbulent and vicious habits of his youth, and had become absolutely dependable.

It took about six and a half hours to run the hundred and thirty kilometers from Strassburg to Manheim, but we were dragging the pilot's heavy tub most of the way, and I do not think that our average running speed ever exceeded twelve kilometers an hour in fresh water. On arriving at Manheim our pilot acted as if he were viewing the city for the first time, and appeared to have no idea of where to find a berth. After he had cut several figures of eight in the swift current looking for some place to dodge in, Ranney became impatient and pointed out his shortcomings with such force and fluency that the man completely lost his head, and would have wrecked us but for a restraining hand. In the end we ran past the town and turned up into the Neckar where we made a good berth and discharged our pilot. He was dangerous to us, and I am afraid that we were becoming dangerous to him.

CHAPTER VIII

THE next morning, having decided that the law regarding Rhine pilots was an injudicious one, we disregarded it and made a good run past Worms and Oppenheim, arriving at the mouth of the Main opposite Mainz a little after the meridian. One could not mistake this river, its water being black as ink from the discharge of the big chemical factories below Frankfort. A very peculiar effect is produced at the line of demarcation where this Styx-colored stream meets the pale yellow water of the Rhine.

The Rhine from Strassburg to Mainz is neither interesting nor scenic. At first one sees the hills of Baden some distance from the river on the starboard side; lower down the country is flat and monotonous. Much more interesting are the powerful towboats plowing up against the swift current with their trim steel barges, whose fast, fine lines would not disgrace a steam yacht.

129

The signal system for boats passing each other on the Rhine and Danube is simple and efficient. The side on which to pass is indicated by a blue flag waved at the end of a long pole from the port or starboard end of the bridge. This signal is answered in the same way, and is unmistakable. The whistle is not used.

We turned up into the Main in company with a number of tows bound for Frankfort, and as there were five locks and we no longer had our " vortfahrtsrecht " privilege so much time was lost in locking through that the darkness came while we were still some miles below Niederad. It was very cheerless. Instead of the *Beaver* lying in a snug berth at Frankfort, and ourselves in a snug berth at the rathskeller, as we had anticipated, we found ourselves plowing up against the current of a strange river with a rocky bed, through the pitch dark in a drizzle of rain. There were bridges and tows and cable ferries and other disagreeable things, but there seemed to be no place to fetch up, so we got out our side lights and held on through the murk wondering how we were going to tell when we got to the place where we wanted to stop. The stern wave presently mounted in a way to indicate shoal water, and Pomeroy took a heave of the lead.

" A scant fathom," says he.

" What's the bottom? "

" Flint rocks, stuck on edge."

We shifted out a little and presently got more water. The river was tortuous and the channel very narrow. Also it was late and we were getting hungry and tired and bored. The night was as dark as a chain locker; you could tell the water from the land and that was about all. The lights on the shore shone flat and blinding through the fine drizzle of rain. Before long I grew discontented.

" We have come far enough to reach that lock," said I. " This is a foolish pastime. Let us creep quietly into the bank and tie up."

" We have got to eat," said Ranney.

That is always a powerful argument, so we held

on at full speed. Presently Pomeroy said, " I will take a sounding."

But there was no need.

Biff.   Bang.   Bump.   Bumpety, bumpety, bumpety, bump! The *Beaver* climbed upon a stone wall, ran along the top for a way, and jumped down into the water on the other side. But she kept on going. Dan didn't care; that was wherein he excelled over the nickel-plated yacht engine. The *Beaver* drew about three feet, but given a good start Dan could take her along in two, for some considerable distance.

" What the dickens was that? "

" A spur of the Schwarz Wald. Never mind."

" What do you think that you are driving? A steam roller or a racing car? " (This to me.)

" Thunderweather!   and I wanting to tie up to that sausage barge back by the last   ."

Biff.   Bang.   Bump!

" Here we come to the Bavarian Alps! Go it, you sixteen-square-head-power tram car! Go 'cross lots if you like! We don't care! "

" Put her at the bank and we'll take the road. It's more direct." (That sounded like the artist.)

" Can't help it, Ranney must have his dinner."

We kept her going. Only a little paint off the big American elm keel. Suddenly the lock loomed up ahead out of the encompassing gloom.

" We were on the wrong side of the river! "

" You cannot be on both sides at once, and there is only one right side to this trickle."

We tied up and then walked halfway across Germany in the dark until we came to a nice little inn, where our vexations were soon forgotten.

When we reached Frankfort the following morning, the first question we asked was about the water in the Main, although we knew what the answer would be.

" *Wasser*? " said the captain of the canal boat, " with that motor boat out of sight of Frankfort to get it is not possible. If a month more early you had come, yes! To-day   nit. Each day it lower gets! "

It was true. Telephoning up the river we learned that owing to the extreme drought of the season the Main was navigable only to vessels drawing under twenty inches, whereas when not under way we drew two feet eight inches, and when running, three feet five inches.

Said Pomeroy: " It's a beaver. She will have to climb the tree."

ACROSS EUROPE IN A MOTOR BOAT

I was secretly glad. Since sailing from London
we had passed through two hundred and twenty-
three locks. I never want to see another lock
except in the Panama Canal.

The problem then was how to get the *Beaver*
into the Danube. We consulted Herr Otto Eberl
of Würzburg, who wanted six hundred marks to
float her up to Bamberg on a scow. That was too
much. Inquiring further, Herr Ignatz Eingartner
contracted to load her on a flat car for one hundred
marks, take her to Regensberg for ninety marks,
drop her into the Danube there for thirty marks.
Insurance at seventeen marks. Total, two hundred and thirty-seven marks.

Since the *Beaver* could not go up the Main and
through the Ludwig Canal, which enters the Danube at Regensberg, on her own bottom, the only
difference that it made whether she went on the
bottom of a scow or the bottom of a flat car was
three hundred and sixty-three marks, which to us
was a powerful factor. We therefore shipped her
across to Regensberg forthwith. There we found
her on our arrival, floating peacefully beside the
bank none the worse for her overland journey, and
in an hour or so we had filled our fuel tanks, rigged
out the stern awning, and got things generally ship-

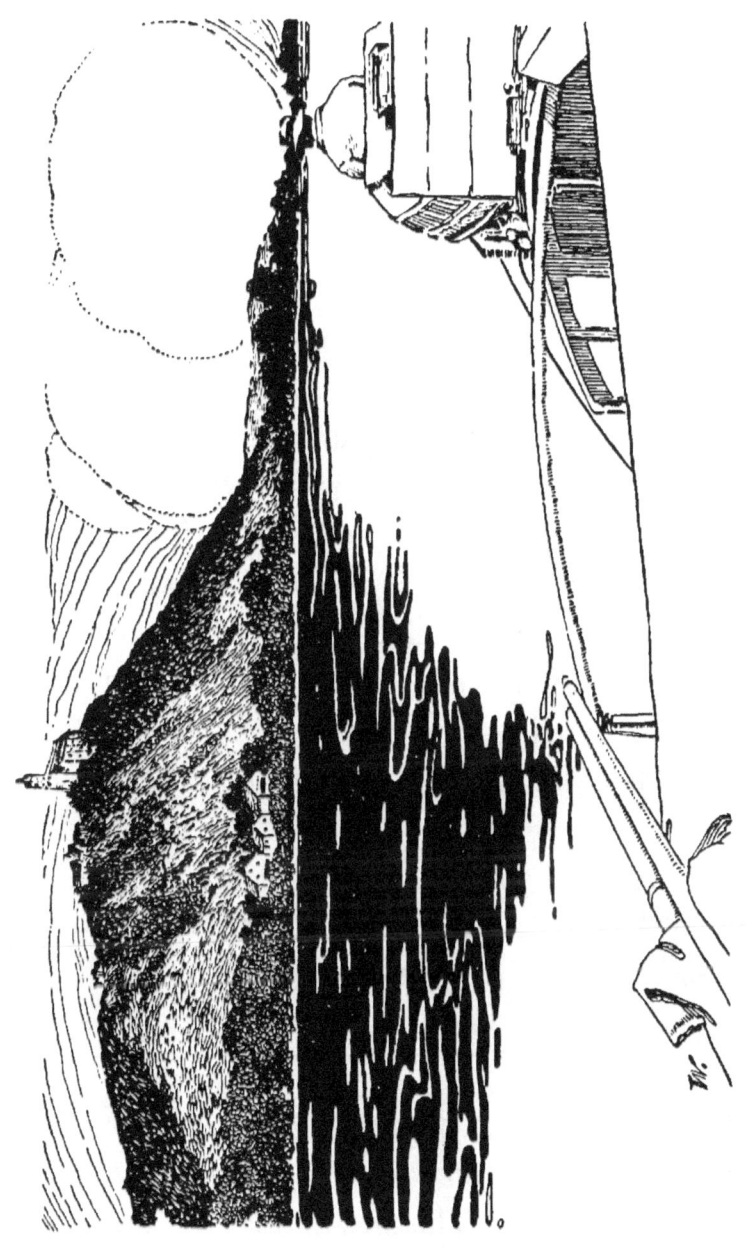

"Onward it goes, skirting kingdoms as it first skirted hamlets."

shape for our little jaunt of nearly fifteen hundred miles to the Black Sea.

The Danube is still a small stream at Regensberg, but the current is swift and, as the channel is tortuous, winding down between shoals and rocky ledges, we were strongly advised to take a pilot, although this was not compulsory by law, except at certain dangerous passages. While discussing the matter among ourselves a bystander informed us that the river was very low, that there were many false channels and shifting sand banks and rocks and waterfalls and cascades and whirlpools and stone dikes, and that without a pilot we would never get beyond the first bend alive. On hearing this Ranney accused him of being a pilot himself, which he admitted to be the fact.

" If we have got to take a pilot for the whole Danube," said Pomeroy, " on reaching Sulina we will have to sell the boat to buy food! "

" The man is a liar," said Ranney, " and he is looking for a job! "

The river looked wet enough to me. Personally I hate pilots, and dislike to have any stranger take charge of my boat. This was particularly the case on the *Beaver*, where it was often necessary to

handle the steering wheel and motor controls together.

It did not take much discussion to decide us to
try it alone. Encouraging Ranney to insult the
prophet of ill we heated up Dan and turned him
over before a wondering audience, little suspect-
ing how near the ill-omened croakings would come
to being fulfilled within the next ten minutes.

In loading the *Beaver* on the car they had set
her down on athwartships skids, deeply notched to
receive the keel. These skids were big balks of
pine about six by four inches square and the width
of the car in length. In two of the skids the
notches cut for the keel fitted closely, the weight of
the boat jamming them hard and fast, so that when
the boat was lifted off the car and lowered into the
water under the crane at Regensberg these skids
had remained attached. A few blows of a maul
would have knocked them clear, but nobody had
taken the trouble, and once in the water the wood
had swelled and jammed even tighter. The water
itself was too turbid to permit of the skids being
seen.

The *Beaver* was lying in rather an awkward
place to get away from as the current was very
swift, her head was upstream and the river too

narrow to turn without going alternately ahead and astern. To complicate things still further the bank just below us was shelving and faced with stone, while a little distance down there was a railroad bridge with a big stone pier in midstream. The river just below was filled with shoals. But although requiring careful judgment the maneuver of turning around under way offered no difficulty with a boat which handled as nicely as did the *Beaver*.

As we started out into the stream it struck me that the boat was singularly unresponsive, which was not altogether strange considering that she was dragging two eight-foot balks of timber athwart her keel, but I ascribed this sluggishness to the force of the current. Working upstream far enough to make the turn and get straightened out before being drifted too close to the bridge pier, I attempted to get around in the usual way, when, instead of swinging as she should have done, she lay heavy and inert, the rudder apparently of no effect and the screw lashing up the water without result.

In vain I put her ahead and astern; she could not seem to gather way enough in the short scope offered by the width of the river to get under control of the wheel, which was very puzzling, as we had

" Winding tortuously between high, thickly wooded hills.''

often spun her around almost in her tracks. We were flying downstream broadside on with disaster looming closer every moment. Pomeroy and Ranney looked around at me inquiringly, but feeling that something was wrong without knowing what it was, kept quiet—a purely Anglo-Saxon accomplishment in a crisis!

To have gone astern would have meant being broken in two across the bridge pier; there was no room ahead of us owing to the shelving wall. We were swirling down on a line of shoals, which had we struck broadside on in a long, narrow boat like the *Beaver*, would have resulted in our being rolled over and over in the swift current. As a last resort I tried jumping the boat ahead suddenly by throwing the throttle wide, and at the same time giving the propeller blades the angle of their fullest thrust. The boat lunged powerfully, there was a bumping under the bilge, a commotion in the water, and up came first one big balk of timber and then another!

" Why, those are the skids! " cried Pomeroy.

" Yes," I answered, " and they nearly skidded us. Another two minutes and they might have brought the keel up with them! "

I do not think that anybody but myself realized

"Each day tells a new and changeful story."

what a close shave that was, especially as the obstacles had been ripped off in time to get the boat
straightened out before reaching the bad water.
Previously to this we had had one close shave in
the Thames at Wapping Stairs, had been in some
danger of destruction when the motor stopped off
the French coast in the Channel, and had also " enjoyed " some twenty or thirty other " exciting incidents." But as a diaphoretic for the man at the
wheel those skids held the record up to date!

Such was our send-off on the long *chute* from

the highlands of Central Europe down to the
sea.

It is a fascinating thing to strike a great river
far up in its course and follow it day after day as
it winds down past mountain and plain, through
rich, fertile valleys, receiving one great tributary
after another, flowing past the moldering remnants
of ancient civilizations, and washing the walls of
busy modern cities. Each day tells its new and
changeful story, until the pretty little river, at the
start scarcely more than a picturesque streamlet
across which a man could almost wade, becomes
a vast, majestic stretch of water from the middle
of which one sees the shores bathed in the blue of
distance. Onward it goes, skirting kingdoms as at
first it skirted hamlets, opening new vistas the
depths of which lie over the horizon, flowing ever
on and into the unknown.

Unknown it proved to us from the very start.
Before Regensberg was a kilometer astern we had
tasted of the uncertainty of swift river navigation,
bouncing over a cobbly shoal and squattering into
the rapids beyond, half in and half out of the water like a wounded duck. A little later, having
absolutely nothing to go by, we took the wrong side
of an island and ran up onto a sand bank, but for-

"Just below Regensberg we passed 'Walhalla.'"

tunately the current was not swift at this point and by shifting our extra drums of fuel and reversing hard we slid off into the deep water again.

The Danube is a queen among rivers. Never in Europe, Asia, Africa, nor the two Americas have I seen its like. The length of that part of its course which we followed, if laid off in a straight line for purposes of comparison would be almost equal to the distance from New Orleans to Winnipeg, but excepting the environments of Vienna and Budapest there was not a single day's run where the scenery failed to be charmingly picturesque while often it was grandly magnificent.

Just below Regensberg we passed " Walhalla," the beautiful " Temple of Fame," a marble palace erected by the mad Ludwig I, King of Bavaria. It rises pure and white and many columned against a background of luscious green on the brink of a hill overlooking the river.

The scenery of all of this part of the Danube is of a delicious, half-wild, half-pastoral beauty, but for the first week we were kept too busy watching the river itself to spend much time in admiration of the valley through which it flowed. Charging down at full speed, with a current which at times we could not have stemmed, and trying to follow a narrow tortuous channel winding through ledges or deflected from treacherous shoals, we had little opportunity for day dreaming. There are many long stretches where the channel is either not indicated at all or if it is, by slender spars which the force of the current keeps submerged. Sometimes a quick bend would present to us a river split into three or four branches running between an archipelago of islands. There was never any time to deliberate on our course. Tearing down as we were the question had to be decided at once and finally. Our charts were useless, being merely land maps. The location of the true channel had to be guessed at, or more accurately determined from the character of the banks and the general expression of the river. Usually this was not difficult, but at certain times taking the true course was a matter of chance. More than once during the day we would drive down into what looked as if it must be the channel suddenly to find ourselves in a *cul-de-sac*, or funnel, where the current swirled down through gradually narrowing banks, finally rushing through a sluice filled with snags, rocks, and shoals. If we discovered our mistake in time we could usually turn and crawl back foot by foot into the main stream; if not, we would throw on the full strength of the motor to get quick steerage way and shoot the rapids. Again, we might travel for kilometers out of the main channel and hidden away behind some island but in perfectly good water, eventually coming out into the river again.

Some of these experiences were very exciting. There was double danger in taking the ground. In the first place, to have struck and swung broadside where the current was swift would have meant being rolled over and over like a log, the boat smashed and ourselves possibly crushed; on the other hand, if we had run aground in some of the remote places between islands and away from the main stream where we sometimes found ourselves, we might have stayed there indefinitely. Such feeble gear as we had aboard would not have moved the *Beaver* if she " went on hard." Owing to the turbid, " absinthe frappé " color we could not see the bottom in over a meter of water, the quickest indication that it was shoaling being the rapidly mounting stern wave. When this began to " comb," our keel was not far from bottom, and the course was then to swing as soon as possible to the side on which the quartering wave was the lower.

"The scenery is of a delicious, half-wild, half-pastoral beauty."

Our first day's run took us up to Deggendorf in Bavaria, where the Danube receives the Isar. Here we found that we were required by law to take a pilot, the passage between this point and Passau being very dangerous. As there was no regular pilot on the spot the local *ruder club* kindly recommended a man whom we took, but who proved to be incompetent. Just below Deggendorf the river roars down in a cataract, through a shallow channel winding among ledges, and twice our pilot bumped us over a rock, which so frightened him that at Vilshofen he completely collapsed and was unwilling to go on. Ranney, the spokesman where German was current, harangued him as follows:

Ranney: Do you call yourself a pilot?

Pilot: Certainly I am a pilot.

Ranney: Hell is full of such pilots! (At least it sounded like that.) Do you think that we are such (German expression not translatable) fools as to pay another fool to bump this boat on the rocks when we can do it ourselves for nothing?

Pilot: The river is very low.

Ranney: That is fortunate! If it were high you would bump us on the roofs of the houses. Other steamers go through without hitting.

Pilot: They draw less water than you do. (This was true.)

Ranney: Do you think that you can go the rest of the way without knocking the bottom out of the boat?

Pilot: It is necessary for me to reflect.

Ranney translated this for me.

" Kick him out," said I, " and let us go on alone. Before we are finished we will wreck this boat trying to obey their silly laws."

Ranney (turning to pilot) : What is the result of your reflection?

Pilot: It has occurred to me that I must ask the permission of the pilot here. This is his part of

"The river scenery is very beautiful."

the river. If he gives me permission I will go on with you.

But that settled it.

"If there is a *real* pilot here," said Pomeroy, "let us get him and chuck this somnambulist out on the beach."

That was what we did. The new pilot, a quiet, businesslike man, took us the rest of the short dangerous stretch to Passau without touching. There, having complied with the law, we paid him off.

CHAPTER IX

THE scenery between Passau and Linz is very beautiful, winding tortuously between high, thickly wooded hills, the Danube Mountains, which are a southern spur of the Bohmer Wald, all of which belong to the Austrian Alps. They rise precipitously, and are often capped by the ruins of mediæval castles, almost indistinguishable from the rocky summits on which they rise. Some of these grim aeries are still in a splendid state of preservation.

At Engelhartszell, about an hour's run from Passau, we reached the Austrian frontier, where we were passed without any questions beyond such as were prompted by the friendly interest taken in our American ensign, flown, as we were told, for the first time on the Austrian Danube from a sea-going vessel.

That night we tied up at Obermühl, a wild, delicious spot where the river narrows to flow deeply between high, thickly wooded hills, sweet with the smell of ferns. We were given a good dinner at an *auberge* on the bank, and the night had the cool freshness of the mountains.

The day following we made a good run which ended sadly. We had left early, stopped for *déjeuner* at Linz, and late in the afternoon disaster overtook us.

Ranney was at the wheel, Pomeroy was forward on lookout, and I was washing some photographic films in the engine room. We were shooting downstream at over twenty kilometers an hour, and for some distance past the river had been fairly open. Suddenly Ranney said, " Where is the channel? "

We were then on the left bank. Looking ahead I saw what I took to be a steamboat landing over the port bow.

" This side," said I. " You are all right."

" Looks like the other side to me," said Ranney.

I studied the river more carefully. At the same moment Pomeroy sang out, " Head over toward that steamboat landing! "

But almost as he spoke we saw a suspicious-looking riffle on the water dead ahead.

" Hard aport! " said I. Ranney spun the wheel

over and at the same moment we touched. Pomeroy had seen the shoal as soon as we and was howling at us to keep off. Knowing that if we once stopped we could never back off against that savage current I reached for the throttle and threw it wide, hoping to drag across as we had done once or twice before. The bar was made up of smooth, round stones about the size of a lemon, and as we had struck it on the edge and at high speed with a slim boat weighing about seven tons it seemed possible that our way might carry us clean across. Our screw was protected by a heavy iron shoe which would take the weight of the stern and receive the rudder post, so there was no danger of damage.

We charged through that gravel bed like an automobile, the boat climbing higher and higher, and if we could have steered her she would have wriggled out into deep water again. But the rudder was straightened out by the gravel through which it plowed and therefore useless. Slower and slower we went, the propeller churning up the cobbles under the stern. Then we stopped. I cut off the motor, and we sat for a moment listening to the roar of the water across the shoal.

" Thunderweather! "

"We are hitched," said Pomeroy. "Here we stop until the winter rains."

There was a steamer coming up far on the other side of the river, and for a moment I was tempted to take in our ensign, not wishing to make a target for ridicule of the only American flag on seventeen hundred and seventy miles of Danube, but decided that the flag was there for good or ill.

"There is no danger of our being run down," said Ranney. "We can sleep in peace."

"What shall we do?" asked Pomeroy.

"It is necessary for me to reflect," said I.

"The river is dropping every day," said Pomeroy, who when not a sanguine optimist is an inky pessimist.

"How much wine is there aboard?" asked Ranney.

"None," said Pomeroy, "and the cobbles are scouring out from under the stern. We are going higher every minute."

I pointed out that such a view was pessimism on a debauch, and that nothing short of a ten-ton crane could put her any higher. By throwing on full power I had already put her as high as she could go. Then I reflected.

Thinking the situation over cheered me up. I

pointed out to the others that we could not have found a better place in which to " pile up " on the whole Danube. The water was clear, the scenery was charming, and the air fine. But there was no pleasing the artist, who began to prick off our

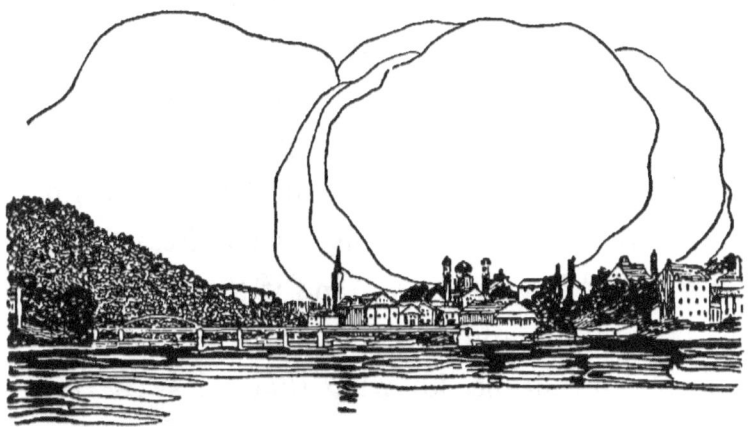

"The water was clear, the scenery was charming."

course and tell us where we would have been at half past seven if we had not struck.

It was then about half past five in the afternoon. We were almost in the middle of the river on the outer edge of the shoal, which reached nearly to the left bank, from which it was separated by a narrow channel. Any attempt to warp off with such light gear as we had aboard was out of the question; our big anchor might have held the boat against the current, but that was about all.

Less than half a mile upstream there was a cable ferryboat, and it seemed most probable that the ferryman would have a big grapnel with hawser and tackle. The proper wrecking operation was obvious: that was, to put the grapnel at the end of a long, stout hawser in the stern of a pulling boat, hang to the ferryboat until she got opposite the *Beaver*, then cast off, drop down with the current, let go the grapnel well upstream, and bring the end of the hawser aboard the *Beaver*. With a good purchase and four or five men to heave, something would have to move, and if the anchor were big enough it might be the boat.

In the meantime, knowing that all swift rivers are capable of quick rises at times from rains higher up, it seemed a good plan on general principles to get an anchor out astern. I had grave doubts of my being able to pull our sampan against the current, but decided to have a try, so we threw her overboard, first taking the precaution to make a heaving line fast to the painter. But pulling my hardest I could not even hold my own, and was whisked downstream and hauled back by the others, incidentally getting capsized in the process.

"That," said Pomeroy, "is a failure."

"It is more. It is a farce."

" What next? "

" Comedy. I will disrobe and walk upstream to the edge of the shoal with the anchor."

That job was like a clog-footed nightmare. The water was only waist deep, but the current was so swift that it took me downstream on the run. With *ski* one could have reached Vienna in time

"Less than half a mile upstream there was a cable ferry-boat."

for dinner. I soon found, however, that with an eighty-pound anchor on one shoulder I could get to windward, but I did not get it far enough, for when we all took a strain we found that we could heave the anchor home through the loose gravel. I tried again, and at the end of half an hour's hard work succeeded in getting it out in slightly deeper water. The others watched me with languid interest.

" Do you need any help? " asked Pomeroy, politely.

" Oh, no; thank you. But do come in; the water
is fine! "

He came and we tried it together, I carrying the
anchor, and the artist behind me and buttressing
us both against the weight of the current with the
boat hook. But it was not a notable success. The
artist was not as " deep draughted " as I, and
twenty years of French cooking and dining out
had increased the dimensions of his submerged section. Once below the Plimsoll mark he went to
leeward fast. In the end I had the anchor in one
hand, the boat hook in the other, and Pomeroy
was hanging to the hawser to keep from going to
Budapest alone. If we had been carried over the
edge of the shoal we would have seen a good deal
of Austria-Hungary before we could have swum to
the bank.

In time we got the anchor out almost to the end
of the cable, went back aboard, and hove taut and
made fast. The artist then produced a bottle of
brandy, which he had procured in London, and kept
hidden and untampered with. We needed it, for
the water was cold.

Ranney and I decided to go ashore in the sampan

"A village on the upper Danube."

and interview the ferry people. This sampan was the little tub which we had built in Pomeroy's studio on the *rue des Sablons*, and was eight feet long by two and a half beam. It had been drying out on the cabin house and leaked like a bait car, but Ranney bailed the water out while I pulled strenuously for the shore. Crossing the channel near the bank it was touch and go, but we arrived, some distance downstream.

Ranney explained our needs to the ferryman, who said that the scheme was the proper one, and volunteered to conduct operations himself the following morning. He showed us a big four-pronged grapnel which might have weighed two hundred-weight, and a hundred and fifty fathoms of good, stout hawser, also a double tackle. He then detailed us a man with one of the long river boats, propelled like a gondola, to go out to get Pomeroy. Accordingly, we hung behind the ferry-boat which tacked across the river, driven only by the force of the current and held in position by a trolley which traveled on a cable swung across up-stream, and when opposite the *Beaver* we cast off and dropped down.

As we glided alongside there issued from the cabin a cheerful burst of song to the music of the " Blue Danube ":

We're pollywogs fine — Bl'p-bl'p   bl'p-bl'p!
We live in ·the slime — Bl'p-bl'p   bl'p-bl'p!

It appears that the artist had continued to fortify his system against the chill of his immersion, and had passed from his state of acute pessimism to one of radiant optimism. But the shadow of calamity still lurked in the background, and as we sculled ashore he said:

" I am cheered up at this moment   but I know that I am going to be awfully sad over this job in an hour or two. We will get off all right

of course   only I do not see how we are going
to do it."

" She is roosting as high as the skysail yard, and
that is no deep-sea pleasantry, but if you could see
that big red ferryboat's hand hook you would
burst into song again."

Our boatman directed us to a tavern where we
found a huge, handsome woman, cooking *schnitzel*
over a charcoal fire. She was a blonde, blue-eyed
Brunhilde, and looked, even while frying *schnitzel,*
as if she had just escaped from Wagnerian opera.
Observing our admiration as she served our beer,
she informed us that she was twenty-five years old,
weighed one hundred kilos (or it may have been
two hundred), and was very lonely, as her husband
was off in the Austrian Tyrol on his military
service.

" Tell her," said I to Ranney, " that if he were
any kind of a man he would desert."

Ranney did so, whereat she smiled at *him*. Then
Pomeroy told her that we were from the motor
boat which was hung up to dry in the river, and
she replied that she had observed our predicament,
and that we would never get the boat off.

" There! " said the artist, pessimist again, " that
is what I told you."

"Tell her," said I to Ranney, "that since we have seen her we don't want to get the boat off."

Ranney told her, and she smiled and turned her blue eyes on *him* again.

"Tell her that *I* said it," I snapped.

"Tell her yourself," said Ranney.

I turned to Pomeroy. "*You* tell her."

"Do not annoy me with such trivial matters," said he. "This is a crisis in our lives."

I saw that his mind had gone back to the boat. I will never again travel through a country the language of which I do not speak and with two companions who speak it fluently.

Brunhilde told us that there was to be a dance that evening, and cordially invited us to the party. Ranney and I accepted and had a very pleasant evening, but a presage of ill had descended upon the artist, who refused to quit the terrace, where he sat in solitude, imbibing large tankards of the spiritless beer of the country. Ranney, who is a very good dancer, made a great hit, and was strongly urged to execute the national dance of America, which they understood to be "dar kak volk."

A little after midnight we bade a qualified good-by to our kind hostess, and when a waiter had hunted up our boatman and dragged him out of his bed, we went down to the river and started out aboard. It was very dark, overcast, and we had neglected to leave a light on the *Beaver,* but our boatman and the sleepy, under-sized boy whom he had brought along to handle the bow pole, knew their work. Cutting across to the edge of the shoal they shoved the long, narrow skiff up against the fierce current for about half a mile, putting us alongside very nicely.

The wrecking crew came off the following morning while we were cooking our breakfast, and placed the grapnel as planned. While we were rigging the tackle the local Herr Strommeister (stream master) came alongside and took command of operations. The men worked quickly and intelligently, getting a powerful purchase on the hawser. Making fast to the heavy samson post, which we had insisted upon having, five hands heaved away, and it was not long before we were afloat again. As the boat slid off stern upstream one hand had to get a sweep over the bow to keep her straightened out as the weight of the current jammed the rudder, and there was danger that she might take a sheer on the hawser, broach to, and capsize. As soon as possible we started the motor, then slipped the cable, and turned around under power, bucking the swift current again with great difficulty.

When we landed the crew at the ferry we asked for the bill.

" But there is nothing to pay ! " said the Strom-meister. " It is a pleasure to assist foreign visitors who find our river of sufficient interest to travel its length in a motor boat ! "

The ferryman said also that we owed him noth-ing, but that if we chose we might give his men a few marks. In the end we recompensed them all, including the ferryman. The Strommeister, be-ing an official, we invited to lunch with us at Melk, which was two kilometers back from the river.

Bidding farewell to our friends in need we got under way at 1 :30, and by 7 :30 had reached Nussdorf, one hundred and eight kilometers be-low Melk and about six kilometers above Vienna, when darkness overtook us. Through the influ-ence of some Austrian friend Ranney had obtained permission for us to lie in the Donau Canal, which passes through the heart of the city. The follow-ing morning we dropped down to the canal, where we met with the first accident resulting in any damage to the boat which had happened since sailing from London.

The Donau Canal enters at right angles with the river, and the gates of the lock are at the end of a U-shaped depression in the bank. Ranney, on presenting his credentials to the Strommeister, was told that the gates would be open for us the following morning at nine o'clock, so that we might go directly in without being obliged to hang off and on in the swift current. Accordingly, a little after nine we ran down, when on rounding the shoulder of the bank I discovered that the lock gates were still shut. As there looked to be dead water in the little hole close up against them, I edged in to lie alongside the wall until the lock should open. But instead of the dead water which I had hoped to find, we were caught in a powerful back eddy and flung violently ahead. It was too late to sheer off, so I reversed hard, and put the helm over in an effort to hit the wall rather than the lock gates.

Pomeroy and Ranney were up forward, and expecting every minute to feel the suck and jar of the reversed propeller and to see the headway checked. In still water we could, in emergency, stop the boat from full headway in twice our length, so neither man even thought of getting a fender over the bow. The result was that we hit the wall a solid bump high up on the stem, bending the stock of our anchor, and springing the sheer strake sufficiently to open up two seams in the forward deck planking. The side planking did not budge, neither did Dan, who weighed a ton and a half, but was set down on bed plates which would have held the engines of a tugboat. The only damage was on deck, as the starboard side must have sprung slightly out, then back again, but the gaping fissures looked very bad indeed, especially as one of the deck planks was splintered its whole length.

At the last moment the two up forward had simply hung on. When we had backed away and got a couple of lines to the wall, Pomeroy came aft shaking his head.

" What was the matter? " he asked.

" I think that we were going too fast."

" You didn't get *me* off! " said Ranney. " I hung onto the samson post! "

" Much damage? " I asked.

" Gawd-o-gawd! " said the artist. " Her bow is crumpled in like a busted accordion, and there is a crevasse in the deck that it makes you frightened and dizzy to look into! "

It would have given us plenty of room to enter if they had opened one of the lock gates, but the lock keeper, who had observed my technique in coming alongside, opened both, and then requested us to let them haul us in by hand. Apparently he was afraid that I would take his lock with me and leave him out of a job.

" What will we do about those open seams? " asked Pomeroy.

" We will wait until we find two stone-laden barges breasted a little apart, and then ram in at our top notch and jam these cracks together again ! "

" At Regensburg," observed Pomeroy, " I received a letter from a friend who said, '   how I envy you drifting idly down on the bosom of that glorious stream.   .' "

" Wish he were here ! "

And so, saddened and chagrined, we entered the stately city of Vienna, reflecting on the fact that our descent of the Danube was only just begun, and that there were still over twelve hundred miles of treacherous river between us and the sea.

CHAPTER X

F you ever go down the Danube in your own boat, do not lie in the Donau Canal while at Vienna. We did, and were tormented by visitors whom, considering their kindly interest, it would have been ungracious to ignore. We lay to the bank near the Maria Theresa bridge, and the curious spectacle of a small sea-going motor boat flying the American ensign in the center of Vienna made us the nucleus of a mob of spectators. Reading, writing, or any relaxation was quite impossible even in the cabin or in the privacy of the cockpit, which could be completely tented off. No formal invitation to come aboard was apparently considered necessary. There would be a scuffle of feet, a jar, a little more mud on the deck, and a genial voice exclaiming in English —of a sort:

" Py chingo! But dis vas a bleasure to see our flac! It iss de feerst times I haf seen mein Ameri-

168

can flac on any vessel in Austria." And then there would be the usual courtesies and explanations and tour of inspection.

Throughout the whole of our trip from London to the bitter end we always made it a point to treat every visitor with the utmost courtesy, no matter how ill timed the call, feeling as it were a certain sense of responsibility to the flag which we were carrying for the first time across Europe on an American vessel, and wishing to leave agreeable souvenirs in our wake. But we soon grew careful in picking out a berth where the populace was unable to ramble on and off the boat as if she were a landing stage. If we had lain in the open river on the outside of a barge, our three days' stop in Vienna would have been much pleasanter.

On September 3d we ran out of Vienna, and without a pilot continued down the river. Before we had got far we took the wrong side of an island and ran down into a *cul-de-sac* which ended in extensive shoals, but with a good deal of difficulty we managed to turn around and shove our way back against the swift current into the channel. This sort of thing was continually happening, and sometimes from a labyrinthine passage in an archipelago of islands we would look far across the river and see a steamer's smoke spouting up from a passage which had looked to us as we approached it like a hair-raising, reef-strewn cataract. Advice obtained in advance almost invariably proved useless to us, as the steamboat people lacked the imagination to appreciate the different conditions between navigating a little motor boat, low in the water but quick of control, and a big steamer, slower to handle, but from the high bridge of which it was much easier to pick out deep water or shoals. For instance, we were repeatedly warned of the danger in making the passage of the Grein between Linz and Vienna, where the river roars through a narrow gorge choked by rocks and islets. But this place, while exciting, from the swiftness of the stream, was absolutely easy navigation for us, the channel being quite unmistakable, and blasted to a depth of three meters, with a width of two hundred and sixty feet. The danger lay in making the sharp turns in the swift current, which, while quick work for a big steamer, was not difficult for us, and we went through without any pilot, and no particular emotion beyond that of admiration for the wonderfully beautiful mountain scenery. On the other hand, we were told that the run from Vienna to Pressburg was all plain sailing.

DOWN THE DANUBE

"Follow the Danube," said a steamboat captain largely, and we followed it through island, across shoals, twisting and turning with the lead going constantly and the propeller reversed as often as ahead, while the recollection of our recent misadventure at Melk loomed sinister in our minds. It is one thing to follow the Danube when you know the channel and are looking down on the shoal spots from a height of thirty or forty feet above the water, and another when you are down so low that it is impossible to tell the ripple made by a flaw of the wind striking down through a gap in the hills from the sand bank on which you are going to stop.

We did not linger to visit the famous battlefield of Wagram, where Napoleon defeated the Austrians in 1809 with a loss on each side of about twenty-five thousand men. We spent the night at Pressburg, where we heard some wonderful Hungarian music (we had crossed into Hungary about eight kilometers above Pressburg). Whenever you hear particularly good music in the Balkans you may be sure that it is of Gypsy origin. This strange, furtive nomadic race is much in evidence in this part of the world, there being 300,000 of them recorded in Turkey-in-Europe alone.

It is difficult to classify the Gypsies ethnolog-
ically. They give one the peculiar impression of
not belonging to the humanity of our world, and
seem almost like inhabitants of some other planet
who have landed on this earth through some mistake, and being unable to adapt themselves, must
continually prowl back and forth like wild, sly,
half-tamed animals in captivity.

It has always puzzled me how to regard the
Gypsy: whether as the degraded remnants of some
once-elevated caste or merely as a pariah people.
Illiterate as they are, utterly uneducated, with no
actual religion, unless it be a sort of mysticism
which they keep closely to themselves, dirty, va-
grant, dishonest in petty ways, utterly untrust-
worthy, they have at the same time some very
elevated qualities. Their devotion to their parents
is equal to that of the Chinese; they are extremely
kind to their little children, and I have been told
by people who knew them well that a Gypsy love
is very capable of reaching sublime heights of
generosity and self-sacrifice. When the affection
of a Gypsy is gained, his fidelity is said to be
absolute and unwavering and cannot be betrayed.
As musicians they are quite marvelous, when one
considers that this faculty is with the Gypsy in

most cases a pure natural gift and not the result
of a talent developed by practice and study. The
bulk of the musicians in the average Hungarian
band—indeed, one may say the best of them—
are usually Gypsies, and I do not think that I have
ever heard such violin playing as that performed
by Gypsies.

Physically they are often beautiful when young,
but senile decay commences at a very early age.
The young people of both sexes are usually perfectly made, so far as one can distinguish through
their rags, with lithe, straight bodies, strong,
graceful, and delicately molded limbs, such as one
might expect in an aristocratic stock, skins like
satin, black, abundant hair, straight and fine in
texture, and lustrous, intelligent eyes in which
there always lurks a gleam of cunning. Gypsy
eyes, although black, are also said to give out the
peculiar flat, green glint observed in the eyes of
the cat, and in moments of anger or excitement,
when the pupil is dilated, become round disks of
lambent green. Gypsy hands and feet are small
and graceful and possess that expression of intelligence which one associates with the hands of
people of a higher mentality who use them with
their brains.

The Gypsies are generally supposed to be of
Hindu origin, and their language is of direct
Sanskrit derivation and contains a great many
Hindustani words. The fact that there was a
large migration of Gypsies from Egypt would
have no particular significance, as they are such
a nomadic people and continually wander from
place to place. All through the Orient the Gypsies are known as Chingeni, which becomes Tsigani
in Hungary, Zingari in Italy, Zigeuner in Germany, and Tsigane in France. The Balkan Gypsies are an absolutely pure stock, which no doubt
accounts very greatly for their fineness of type,
the simple reason for this being that they are held
to be utter pariahs of the lowest caste, and no
other race will have any physical contact with
them. This seems strange and inexplicable when
one considers the singular beauty and fascination
of the young Gypsy women, many of whom are
absolutely lovely when judged from any stand-
point of feminine charm, whether of East or West.
There seems to be some deep, underlying natural antipathy, some cosmic incompatibility which
inhibits the attraction of a seductive Gypsy girl
for even so low caste a creature as a Kurd ha-
mal. People I have asked to explain this merely

shrugged and said that it was so. There appears to be also a superstition that tragedy invariably follows in the wake of Gypsy love.

Although the Gypsies in Constantinople appear to have a fairly permanent abiding place, they nevertheless spend a good deal of their time in wandering about the Peninsula, returning to their malhallah for the inclement season. Among themselves they appear to have no organization beyond that of family, no code of morals as we understand the meaning of the word, no organized religion, since they calmly adopt that of the country in which they happen to be—a delicate attention which deceives nobody. In Turkey they are listed as Mohammedans, although observing none of the forms of Islam. The good-natured Turks seem to regard the Gypsies with the same indifferent indulgence as they do the dogs of Constantinople, nor does the government rate them as responsible human beings. The men are exempt from military service and the women never become inmates of Turkish harems. On the other hand, the Turks enjoy the Gypsies' music, often patronize their soothsayers, some of whom appear to be gifted with occult powers of a very advanced degree, and often go to see their dance, which is a very picturesque and interesting sight and should not be missed by any visitors to Constantinople.

The beauty of the Gypsy women is very transient. They mature at the age of ten or twelve, are in their prime from fifteen to eighteen, are old at twenty, and hags at forty, in which condition they remain for any length of time, until a hundred, I was told, which I can readily believe, as I have myself seen Gypsy women who did not look to be a day under three hundred!

We took a pilot the next day for the passage of the Moravian Gate, where the Danube finds its way between the Alps and Carpathians. Farther down the river breaks up into a maze of branches flowing between a labyrinth of islands known as "Schüteen," which cover an area of about six hundred square miles. In such a place as this it is not difficult to lose one's way. Between Pressburg and Gonyo there have been extensive works since 1885 for the maintenance of a navigable channel. Very often these consist of stone dikes built out into any part of the river for the purpose of deflecting the current or keeping the greatest force in the channel, and as these dikes were sometimes submerged several feet and were apt to run straight out from either bank, longitudinally, transversely, or diagonally, often in the very middle of the stream, it was quick and nervous work to locate them in water the whole of which was a mass of swirls and eddies.

We discharged our pilot at Komorn, and the following day made a run of one hundred and twenty-five kilometers to Budapest. Just beyond Komorn at Waitzen the Danube makes its big rectangular turn to the south and flows away straight down the meridian of 19° east for about one hundred and sixty miles. We found the current much less swift as we entered upon this part of the course, which is across the plains of Hungary, and for the first time since leaving Regensburg were able to enjoy a little relaxation.

Remembering our social trials in Vienna we ran straight through Budapest looking for a good berth, then turned and worked back upstream, and eventually stopped at the Pannonia Evezös Rowing Club, where we asked permission to tie up. This was most readily granted, and the members showed us every courtesy, putting us up at the club-house and doing everything to make our visit agreeable. They were very much interested in our trip and gave us abundant information, not all by any means reassuring, concerning the journey ahead of us to the Black Sea. One of their crews had rowed down to the Sulina mouth of the Danube, a distance of about one thousand five hundred and seven kilometers, or about nine hundred and forty-two miles, the previous year. They told us that lower down we would come to reaches of the river where if the day were slightly hazy we should be able to sight no land, and that as we were approaching the change of seasons we ran great danger from the violent wind storms which broke upon these vast stretches, and were often so terrific that big tugs and steamers were compelled to run for the nearest shelter. They even went so far as to say that they did not think the *Beaver* would live in one of these gales, as the wind blow- ing straight up against the current made the wick- edest sea imaginable. They also cheered us up by warning us with perfect good faith not to land on the Bulgarian side except at towns, as the people were savage and predatory. However, we had by this time grown impervious to warnings. Since leaving London we had been warned of the traffic dangers on the Thames, the treacherous Estuary, the classic perils of the Channel, the appalling Mascaret, or bore from Havre, extending fifty- four miles up the Seine to Duclair, the traffic dan-

Budapest.

gers of locks and canal tunnels five kilometers long, and the current and shoals of the Rhine, and all the rest of it. As somebody said:

" The farther we get, the more dangerous this job gets. By the time we reach the Mediterranean we shall have formed the habit, and when we get back to Paris the driving of a racing car or the experimentation of an aëroplane will be a dull and monotonous way of passing the time."

Personally I was beginning to hunger for a little dull monotony!

We spent a day and a half in Budapest, then accompanied by the good wishes of the rowing club made an early start for the run southward across the plains of Hungary.

Below Budapest we found much less current and a bigger channel. The Danube had by this time received, besides numerous smaller streams, the rivers Iller, Lech, Isar, Enns, Raab, on the right bank, and on the left bank the Altmuhl, Naab, Regen, March, Waag, and Gran, and before we reached Belgrade it was also to receive the three great rivers, Drave and Save on the right bank, and the Theiss on the left. The latter great stream rises high up in the Carpathians, where they separate Galicia and Hungary, and for the lower part

"Some of these grim eyries are still in a splendid state of preservation."

of its course passes through such a flat country that
a rise of thirteen feet in the Danube causes it to
flow backward for eighty-seven miles. The Theiss
is navigable by steamers as far as Tokaj, the Drave
to the confluence of the Mur, and the Save to Sis-
sek, at the confluence of the Kulpa. Some of the
other tributaries, although navigable, are not navigated by steamers owing to their shifting channels;
among these are the Morava, Waag, Gran, Inn,
and Sio. But it is doubtful if even a swift passenger steamer could plow up against the swift currents of the Waag and the Inn. For the same
reason none of the branches of the Theiss is ever
navigated by steamers, although many are navigable for a long distance.

As the river broadened the dangers of navigation became much less, but the difficulty of keeping
in the main stream increased, especially in the early
mornings when the drifting haze obscured the surface of the water, hiding the channel buoys, which
occurred at long intervals, and making it impossible to distinguish islets from the mainland.

Below Budapest the river flows across a vast and
widely desolate country. It is claimed by some
authorities that the plains of Hungary were once
covered by a great fresh-water lake half as big as

the Adriatic Sea, and that this lake was eventually drained by its outlet cutting through the Carpathians at the Iron Gate. The broad plains roll away to infinite distance, sometimes in a gray, undulating country, giving pasture to great herds of horses or the big, white, wide-horned Hungarian cattle. Here and there the smoke from some herder's hovel rises in gusty swirls; on the blue horizon loom the broken outlines of mountain ranges dim with distance. Often the wind comes sweeping across these *puzstas*, heralded by distant clouds, striking the water with such violence as to create a local disturbance which looks like the commotion caused by the current over reefs or shoals.

When the air is clear one may look far across the plain, see the grim, square tower of some ancient Hungarian feudal castle, as it rears bleakly from a commanding eminence. For miles the banks are fringed in willows, which cover also the multitudinous isles and give to the voyager the impression of passing down through interminable willow forests. Wild-faced herders, fishermen, and river folk are often seen prowling the banks; they are savage-looking creatures, sometimes clad in heavy sheepskins, the wool turned inward, with *kalpaks*, or caps of fur, rawhide moccasins, and

puttie leggins of the same material. Frequently
they are Mohammedans, in fez and trek and kaftan or pelisse, once gaudy of color, now weather-
worn to a neutral tint.

On the day of our leaving Budapest we ran well
until half-past four, when we got a hot bearing,
due to our own negligence in not filling the oil cups,
and to avoid all risk we anchored in the river for
the night. It was a beautiful place, resembling a
vast lake in the forest. As the twilight deepened
innumerable water fowl feeding in lakes near by
came down to the river to sleep. We were lying
to our ketch anchor in a sheltered cove behind a
heavily wooded island. Not far away there was
a sand bar, and this was soon covered with aquatic
birds of all descriptions, and their conversations
and complaints continued through the gloaming
and until after the setting sun had shot its last
gleams through the tracery of willow branches on
the western bank, and the full moon looking up
over the forest sent a pale green pathway shimmering across the still water.

Nothing but the experience of them can convey
any impression of the wonderful beauty of the
mornings on the Danube. The dawn comes with
a crimson glow above a thin blanket of baffling

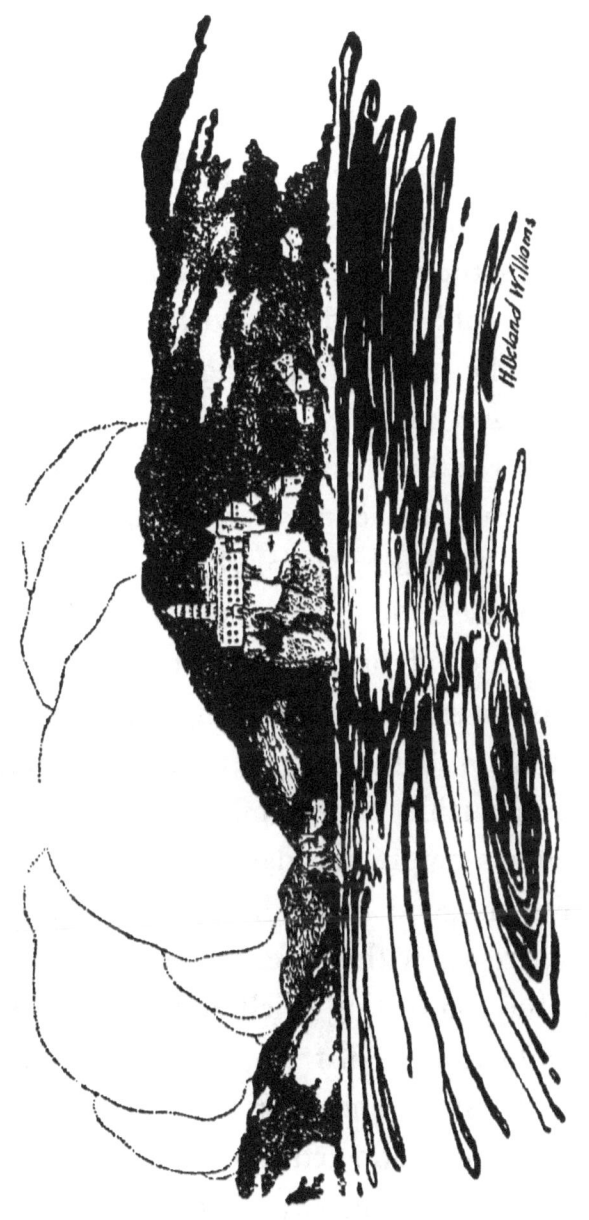

Hungarian Castle on the Lower Danube.

H. Roland Williams

185

mist. Bird cries from all about: the liquid whistle of curlews, and the clear, keen, fifelike notes of snipe and plover. Ducks and fish crows talking sleepily from some invisible sand bank close aboard. The splash of a big fish alongside, then, as the sun rises, the mist seems to thicken, and turns from silver to gold. Suddenly a vista appears, and a glimpse of the river, a dazzling mirror leading through a vague, misty effulgence straight to the sun, a Jacob's ladder without the steps. Queer effects of mirage sometimes obtained, the river seeming to lead upward at an angle, or again downward at a giddy slant. The sun mounts higher; mazy paths lead off hither and yon through the mist; the distant shore reveals itself, to be instantly blotted out again, but it has given us our bearings, and time is valuable, for we must make two hundred kilometers before the darkness comes again. A sweater feels good in the keen air, and a pipe tastes better, even with the aromatic odor of the coffee and the comforting smell and sizzle of frying eggs and bacon. All fresh, vigorous senses of life and action strike chords in these first few moments between sleep and active motion. The smell of the fragrant morning air, the torn lace fringes of the mysterious night rent in the forward thrust

of the awakening day. It is the thin line where
dreams and actions meet. One turns from a con-
templation of the sun-tinted mist to crank the

A mediæval Turkish fortress on the Danube near Ilok.

motor; the fragrance of the river is lost in appetiz-
ing odors from the frying pan. With a prelim-
inary shiver one plunges head first into Jacob's ladder to emerge tingling with other sensations than
those of artistic appreciation., Then *chug* goes
the motor, the water swirls under the stern, one
hand forward to get in the anchor, and we are
slipping off into the dissipating vapor for the
conquest of another fraction of the interminable
river.

The following night we pulled up at Ilok in
Croatia. In the log book I find only this resentful
comment on the place:

"At the hotel we were stung in the bill, which

would not have happened if we had been in Hungary on the other side of the river."

"*A bas Croatia! Vive l'Hongrie!*" We touched this one point of Croatia and Slavonia, and were swindled for the only time on the Danube. What is the result? Croatia will preserve always in our minds a tainted memory. For thus ever does the traveler receive his impressions!

From Belgrade to Sulina the Danube forms a part of the northern boundary of that geographical division of the European Continent known as the Balkan Peninsula. By including the river Save, which joins the Danube at Belgrade, as a part of this boundary, we have allotted to the Balkan Peninsula the following countries or "States," as they are sometimes called: a part of Croatia and Kustendland, Bosnia, Herzegovina, Servia, Bulgaria, a part of Roumania, Montenegro, Eastern Roumelia, Turkey in Europe, and Greece. The term "Balkans" is slipshod and inaccurate, and may be taken to mean either the Balkan Mountains or the Balkan States, which are properly, when spoken of in this way, limited to Servia, Bulgaria proper, Turkey in Europe, Montenegro, and Greece, with Roumania sometimes included. It would seem that the geographical division were

a better one, as these countries present such extreme social, political, and racial differences.

Many people who are comparatively well traveled possess but a very vague idea of what is to
be found in the Balkan Peninsula aside from the
" trouble " which is usually assumed to exist there,
and which usually does! There is a good deal of
difficulty attached to traveling about the interior
of this fascinating whirlpool of the races. Greece
is, of course, well known, but the other countries
are not. Unless one belongs in fez and kaftan, if
a man, or yashmak and feridje, if a woman, the
Mohammedan part of the Peninsula, which in-
cludes all of Turkey and a great deal of Bulgaria,
will be found inhospitable and suspicious of the
stranger. Constantinople and its environs one
may, of course, visit, because the Sultan cannot
very well help it, but for the rest of Turkey there
are no facilities, barring the railroad, which crosses
it. There are no telephones, no automobiles, no
speakable languages, no Baedeker.

It is very unfortunate that there should be such
difficulty in penetrating so beautiful a country as
the valley of the Maritza in eastern Roumelia
and many of the lovely passes and basins of the
Balkan Mountains. There are a number of good

roads and the people are not troublesome, but the inhabitants of the Balkan Peninsula as a whole come of such varied stocks and are so intermingled and colonized within neighboring localities that one needs a host of unheard-of languages in order to get about. The tongues in more common use are Turkish, Bulgarian, Roumanian, Greek, Kutzo-Wallachian, Serbo-Croatian, which is often incorrectly called Servian and is a very widely spoken language, and the Chingeni of the Gypsies. Other languages occasionally spoken are the dialects of Bosnia and Herzegovina, Armenian, Georgian, Yiddish, Hungarian, Circassian, Polish, and Russian. Besides these few mentioned one finds along the coast the languages of the Levant, while Arabic and Persian are affected by the better educated Mohammedan element. English is never spoken anywhere, even in the larger towns where the current language of western Europe would be French or German. We were told that no three languages would be enough to enable a man to travel about without inconvenience in the interior.

The first Balkan country which one reaches in going down the Danube is Servia, a kingdom the area of which is about one half the size of our new State of Oklahoma. Servia is a country of steep hills and mountains often covered with dense forests of beech and oak and fir. Some of these mountains reach a height of 6,000 to 7,000 feet, and the valleys between are rich and fertile, and grow maize, which is the principal food staple; wheat, which is shipped down the Danube to Sulina; and also rye, barley, flax, hemp, and excellent tobacco. In the northeast and east the slopes are planted in vineyards, and we found the native red wine very good, although stronger than that of France and Germany. In the big forests of the west and southwest there are great herds of swine and sheep and goats. One of the principal industries of the country is plum growing.

The true Servians, or Serbs, form about ninety per cent of the total population and are a Slavic people who settled in the country about the middle of the seventh century. Until 1389, when conquered by the Osmanli Turks, they were a very powerful tribe, disputing the domination of the Balkan Peninsula with their neighbors, the Bulgarians. Although sullen and treacherous, they have always been warlike and patriotic, and during the four hundred years of Turkish tyranny there was never a time when they were entirely subjugated and when there was not a guerrilla warfare being waged against their oppressors by patriotic bands of Servians who came down from the inaccessible fastness of the Kopaonik Mountains. The lonely monastery of Studenica was always a headquarters of Servian insurrection.

The religion of Servia is that of the Greek Orthodox Church, and they possess a communistic social organization, called the Zadruga, which is a purely patriarchal system of holding property and dividing labor and the profits thereof.

Servia, like all the rest of the Peninsula, is rich in coal and minerals; but, like Turkey, she is jealous of foreign promoters, and there does not appear to be any development of these natural resources. As a matter of fact, your Servian is a good deal of a barbarian, and, unlike the Roumanian, Bulgarian, and Turk, does not impress one as being yet quite ripe for the arts of peace. By nature he is savage and revengeful, a creature of fierce passions, which he has learned how to conceal, and not quite civilized, as we understand the word. The measures adopted in forming their present dynasty and the indifferent acceptance of the cold-blooded double murder of the late king and queen would sufficiently indicate this.

The national music shows the savage and subdued melancholy which one might expect from the
history of the nation. It is pitched for the most
part in minor key, and when not gloomy is apt to
be frenzied and barbaric. The " hora," the national dance, is wild and passionate. We could
not learn that Servia had produced anything of
art or literature, and the language is still written
in Cyrillian characters, a calligraphy invented and
taught by St. Cyril, the " apostle of the Slavs,"
who died in 869.

Belgrade, the capital city, has had a sanguinary
history, having withstood seven hard sieges. This
" white city," as its name Bielgorod signifies, oc-
cupies a strongly strategic position on a high bluff
at the angle formed by the Save and Danube.
Until the end of the eleventh century it was held
by the Byzantine emperors. After being constantly fought over by Greeks, Bulgarians, Servians, and Turks, it became, in the middle of the
fifteenth century, the bone of contention between
Turks and Hungarians, and during the following
four hundred years was continually changing
hands. The most famous siege was the storming
of Belgrade, and its capture by the Hungarians
under Hunyadi Janos and Capistrano in 1456.

Another important battle was that of August 16, 1717, when Prince Eugene, besieging Belgrade, gained a victory over a relieving army of 200,000 Turks, upon which the city capitulated. In 1862 it was made the capital of the Servian kingdom, and was evacuated by the Turks in 1867.

Next to Belgrade in size and importance is the town of Nissa, where the Emperor Constantine the Great was born 272 A.D.

Approaching Belgrade we saw a curious sight. The banks were very high and bare; behind them appeared to be tumbling hills almost destitute of vegetation. Looking shoreward we saw what seemed to be a black ball rolling with incredible swiftness down a steep fissure in the bluff. Another followed it; two more; a dozen, a score, a hundred, then a multitude of these black rolling objects pouring endlessly down the gully and across the beach to the water, where they collected in solid masses. But still they came, like marbles rolling down a trough, and it was not until we had got our glasses on them that we discovered them to be thousands of black pigs coming down to drink. Hot on their heels came a like number of gray, fluffy balls, which proved to be sheep. They did not mix with the pigs, and I noticed that they were careful to get upstream of them.

This reminds me of another incident which oc-curred farther down the river. As we were plow-ing along we saw two men in a boat some distance ahead, who appeared to be in a mass of *débris*

"We found the whole Danube to be an aviary of water fowl."

which stretched almost from bank to bank. As we drew near we were puzzled to make out what the stuff was. Hundreds of polished stakes pro-jected from the surface of the water and seemed to be drifting slowly toward the bank. Coming closer we saw that it was a big herd of Hungarian cattle changing pasture by swimming from one bank to the other, and what had puzzled us were the horns, which, until we were quite close, were all that were visible.

While speaking of animals I might mention the birds. We found the whole Danube to be an aviary of water fowl. Near Regensburg the marshes were covered with plover, and there were a great many different varieties of ducks which continued all the way down the river. We also saw a great many of the big sickle-billed curlew, wild geese, occasionally wild swans, and snipe of many varieties. In the lower Danube we would sometimes see flocks of from five to twenty big, long-legged, short-billed birds, which from a distance resembled cassowaries, but which I made out through the glass as the European bustard. In the marshes approaching Sulina there were a great many pelicans. Sea gulls fly straight across Europe from the Atlantic Ocean to the Black Sea. We saw the great gray gull and the small tern in the Seine, the Marne, the Rhine, the Main, and the whole length of the Danube. As the head waters of the Rhine and Danube rise almost together in the vicinity of Lake Constance, I have no doubt that the gulls fly up one water way and down the other. Sometimes in going down the Danube we would come upon great sand bars of an area of several acres, where it did not look as if one could step without trampling some sort of water fowl. I have never seen such quantities anywhere with the exception of Lake Menzaleh in Egypt. I did not see any flamingoes on the Danube, but thought once or twice that I saw ibis.

CHAPTER XI

T happened to be the king's birthday when we arrived in Belgrade, and, while we were there, there happened to be a very magnificent funeral. If one remembers, this monarch's accession to power was the occasion of a *not* very magnificent double murder. Servians with whom we discussed the tragic assassination of the former king and queen were inclined to merely shrug and say that, after all, that had proved to be the best way out of a bad business. Beyond Budapest, where East is supposed to meet West, one finds the usual Oriental lack of veneration for human life as such. Your Mohammedan will be much more ready to kill his brother if circumstances seem to justify it, than he will be to kill a cat or dog.

Belgrade is situated on the top of a hill, and from the fortress one gets a magnificent view

" A series of precipitous rocky gorges."

across the lower Hungarian plain and of the Save, which enters the Danube here. For the next sixty miles before entering Roumania, at the Iron Gate, the Danube flows through a series of precipitous, rocky gorges with the Servian highlands on the right and the Transylvanian Alps, a part of the Carpathian system, on the left. The first great defile begins at Golubatz and reaches almost to Dobra. We had wired from Orsova for a pilot, and on leaving Belgrade ran down alone to Alt Moldova, where we spent the night. At this place we made the acquaintance of the school-teacher, who treated us very kindly, and gave us a great deal of useful information. It was odd to find tucked away in this wild recess of the mountains a man of such intelligence and education as our friend; also it was pathetic, especially when we told him we were bound for Constantinople, and he said with a sigh:

" To think that you have come from London, and are going to Constantinople, and appear to treat it as nothing out of the ordinary. Do you know that it has been the dream of my life to see Budapest! " And we were only four days' run from Budapest!

Our friend the school-teacher told us that there

was a pilot in the next room, and a few minutes
later excused himself and returned with a crisp,
confidence - inspiring Hungarian, properly uni-
formed and certificated. He told us that our having engaged a pilot at Orsova would make no difference, as they all belonged to the same company,

The Iron Gate.

and that he would take us down the Kazan-Klause
and through the Iron Gate. Accordingly he came
aboard the next morning, and we started. The
pilot whom we had engaged was waiting for us at
Drenkova, so we stopped to pick him up and took
him on as a passenger. The two pilots were so
pleased with the *Beaver*, and the beautiful delicacy
with which she handled, that they squabbled all the

way like two schoolboys in regard to whose turn it was to steer.

At Drenkova the Danube enters the second or Greben defile, the Upper Klisura, immediately after which one enters the rapids of Izlas, the Lesser Iron Gate (Gornje Demir Kapu), formed by the reefs of Tachtalia and Izlas, and quite distinct from the true Iron Gate below Orsova. After this Lesser Iron Gate comes the marvelously magnificent gorge of the Kasan-Klause or Lower Klisura. Several kilometers beyond, at Old Orsova, comes the rock-ribbed passage generally known as the Iron Gate.

This stretch of the Danube from Belgrade to Turnu-Severinu is traversed by passenger steamers, and is without doubt the grandest spectacle of its kind which Europe has to offer. The great Danube is in places constricted to what did not look to be more than a hundred meters in width, of unsounded depths, and sluiced between lofty precipitous walls of granite and Jurassic limestone. One passes successively from swift-winding defiles into silent basins hemmed in by the great Carpathians, and from which no outlet is visible.

Running rapids in a motor boat is great sport, as in addition to the speed of the current one keeps the motor going "top notch," so as to have the quickest response to the helm. Glancing down at the water we seem to be at our normal speed, but a look at the precipitous mountain side shows us to be flying.

Presently, driving full at a sheer rocky rampart,

"Lofty, precipitous walls of granite."

there appears a narrow fissure and a glimpse of white, tumbling waters at which the boat is dashing full speed.

"The gentleman up forward had better hold tight," says the pilot. "It is also possible that he may get wet."

"The gentleman up forward" has seen the broken water and needs no advice. The *Beaver* is caught in the suck, rushes forward with giddying speed, her high, sea-going bows plunge into the stationary waves, a back swash from the rocky rampart spins her head, the pilot catches her with the wheel, back comes the eddy from the other bank, and the " gentleman up forward " grips the samson post and thinks of the defective steering gear which has already parted so many times, and is destined to part once more. The towering rocky walls, with their deep, gloomy caverns, mount straight from the stream, cut off the vivid daylight, and fill the place with the subdued tints of twi-light. Then suddenly a broad vista opens ahead, and we shoot out into another sheltered lake of wild and romantic beauty.

Just above the Iron Gate, opposite an island in the river, which oddly enough is still occupied by a Turkish garrison, although tucked away between Servia and Roumania, there is a signal station warning vessels when to make the passage of the Iron Gate. The cataract itself tumbles over a rocky ledge of jagged, saw-tooth points, extending for about a mile, and which formerly could only be crossed when the river was high. Now, how-ever, there is a sluice built between stone walls, through which one passes swiftly but in safety,

and down which we coasted with a sensation of
" shooting the chutes."

Throughout the whole length of the series of
gorges through which we passed we saw traces on
the right bank of the causeway built by the Emperor Trajan, whose epoch was from 98 to 117
A.D. In certain places the limestone was hewn
out of the sheer cliff; in others, where the forma-
tion was of granite, there were deep, square holes
sunk at regular intervals in the face of the rock,
evidently to support timbers along which the causeway was built. As the road preserved a regular
elevation of about ten feet above the river, and had
been built on the side where the walls were more
regular and the water deeper, it looked as if it had
been intended for a towpath rather than a causeway. There is also a Trajan memorial cut in the
face of the rock near Orsova.

At Turnu-Severinu we discharged our pilot, the
last we had on the Danube, finishing the run of
about four hundred and seventy-two miles to Sulina under our own direction. For the most part
this was not difficult, as the channel from the Iron
Gate to the mouth is well buoyed with black and
red cans, which one follows as at sea. But from
now on the country was very wild and desolate,

with towns and villages few and far between, and great reaches more like the sea than a river. Also we encountered daily morning mists in which one was for a time quite lost, and it was necessary to keep the lead going constantly, as shoals were apt to be found in any part of the stream. At about ten of the morning the mists would blow away and the wind come up the river with great violence. I remember one morning when, on taking a short nap in the cabin, I awakened to find the boat jumping almost clean out of the water and throwing the spray clear over the cabin house. There were some days when the wind, sweeping down the river, would knock up a sea which delayed us considerably. Being behind our schedule we would not make our day's destination any particular place, but would plow ahead as long as the daylight held, and then edge into the bank and drop anchor in some secluded little bight among the islands, where we should have shelter from any quick, violent blow, a necessary precaution, as there is no holding ground anywhere.

These were delightful days, as we were not under constant strain, and had time to attend to some of the little details of cruising life, such as laundry, mending clothes, writing letters, developing photo-

An old Fortress on the Danube.

graphs, and the like. We stopped for supplies at different towns, Palanka, Ostrovie-Battu, and places without names which we could spell or pronounce. It is difficult for an Anglo-Saxon to convey the name of the village, such as " Srnktzvl," but there were several which sounded like that, or worse.

Fortunately we were after the mosquito season, and never had use for our elaborate system of nets, or, better yet, our quinine. All of this part of the Danube is terribly fever-ridden, and the inhabitants show it in their appearance.

Here is the log of one day verbatim:

" Head of Ostroviel Strimbu Mare. Saturday, September 14th. Clear. Heavy mist over water. Advanced the time fifty-five minutes after Oltenitza. Fetched by Giorgivu, and stopped at Intrakan (Bulgaria) to buy stores. Could not make ourselves understood, and they would not take Austrian money. Finally got hold of the Hungarian Company's steamship agent (who spoke French), and he kindly changed our money, and also accompanied Abe and Hank to make various purchases. Ran until dark. Charming evening, and we have had a most delightful day. We are muchly cheered by a most delightful smell coming

from the stew pot on the stove. After dinner a
tow came plunking upstream, slowed down for the
shoal, passed just above us, kept their lead going,
and crawled slowly ahead.

"Remarks:

    5.40. Got the anchor.

    7.30. Rutchschuk.

" 12.20. Intrakan.

" 12.35. Oltenitza.

    7.00. Let go under head of island.

" Distance. 210 kilometers."

By this time we were well known on the river.
Steamers going both ways had reported us, and
everywhere we met with the kindest and most hospitable treatment imaginable. The swift passenger steamers would give us a friendly dip of the
ensign in passing, and in crossing from one country into the next we had no difficulty nor delay.
Our passports had been viséd for Roumania, Bulgaria, and Turkey, which was all that was necessary, as the other countries do not require them,
and we did not need to enter Russia. As for languages, we had command of French, English, German, Spanish, and Italian. French and German
alone will carry one from Havre to Constantinople, on our route, but a mere smattering would not

do. Both must be spoken and understood thoroughly, as it is often necessary to converse with people who speak them poorly, in argot or with a strong foreign accent. English is quite valueless. One never hears nor has occasion to speak it. As far as I could discover, it is the only European language not spoken on the Balkan Peninsula.

In this lower part of the Danube we found little or no current, and the wind, as in most rivers, blowing directly up and down, never across, following the stream in all of its windings. The local traffic takes advantage of this fact, and we passed fleets of great lumbering vessels, which reminded me strongly of some of the light-draught junks I had seen upon the rivers in China. They never tacked, but waited for a fair wind. The breeze was usually up the river in the morning and downstream in the afternoon. These vessels were of nondescript rig, often two-masted, setting courses, topsails and topgallant sails on the main and a fore-and-aft sail on the mizzen; some carried head sails. Before a fresh breeze they would boom along like great bowls, making good speed. Their crews were a savage-looking gang of pirates, Mohammedans mostly, if one were to judge by the fez and terk or turban bound around it. The helmsman, standing on the high poop with the long tiller between his knees, was a picturesque figure, as were they all, but if we had anchored among a fleet of these vessels I am inclined to think that an anchor watch would have been kept all night.

"Fleets of great lumbering vessels."

Dan, our motor, had done noble work on the Danube, and during the fifteen hundred miles' run from Regensburg to Sulina never once stopped. He pounded along hour in and hour out, strongly and cheerfully, starting always at the first heave on the crank, and needing no care beyond that re-

quired by any motòr. We had fed him American
oil at first, then a very good American oil refined
in France and Germany, and later a nasty brown
Roumanian product, which apparently he liked better than any diet so far. Later on he got the best-
looking oil of all, the Russian oil from Batoum,
which, strangely enough, he seemed to find too
anæmic, but then Dan was a husky, sea-going,
Danish brute, and he liked a strong, sea-going diet.
Sometimes we forgot to oil him, but it made no
difference; he hammered along just the same, and
then, if we still neglected him, would warn us of
our carelessness by beginning to growl and swear.
He would run hot or cool, wet or dry, with the
propeller in the water or buried in a cobble bank;
it really made no difference to him, and never
seemed to hurt anything. Dan was put together
to stand just the sort of a racket which we gave
him, and he was as economical as a French *femme
de ménage.* The price of his fuel did not vary
much, and the actual daily cost of running the
motor, fuel, lubricating oil, and all, was about
forty cents per hour.

Off Arriavoda, which is where the railroad from
Kustendje crosses the Danube after following
Trajan's wall, which runs from the Danube to the

"A sailing vessel of the lower Danube."

Black Sea, Dan stopped for the first time without orders, but it was not his fault, as the tanks had run dry. We stopped under the railroad bridge, which is, we are told, the highest or longest, I forget which, in Europe, and filled the tanks from our extra supply, and went on to Braila, which we reached at six of the evening.

On approaching Braila, which is the great wheat port of Roumania and second only in importance to Odessa, we came upon hundreds of fine iron grain barges, and a little later sighted the shipping.

The kingdom of Roumania has an area about equal to that of the State of New York. If we are to take the Danube as the northern geographical boundary of the Balkan Peninsula, only a small part of Roumania would be included in this division, but this country is usually thought of in connection with the " Balkan States."

Roumania impresses one as an exceedingly promising country. The bulk of it lies in fertile plains under extensive cultivation and producing splendid crops of wheat and maize, which, we were told, was of a grade superior to the Russian cereal. Bordering the river there stretched great prairies of pasture land, where we saw herds of the magnificent big, white native cattle. To the north, on the slopes of the Carpathians and Transylvanian Alps, there are splendid forests where extensive lumber operations are carried on under the German system of forestry, by which the replanting keeps pace with the felling of trees. Roumania is also very rich in minerals and produces a petroleum of a high grade of combustion. It is a peculiar oil of an old-gold color, and we had been told to avoid it, as it was of inferior quality; but, whatever its qualities under analysis, we got better results with it in our motor than any fuel which we used on the entire trip—far better than from the Russian oil which we used later.

One does not hesitate to predict a very bright future for Roumania, as, besides its great natural resources, the country is extremely well governed and very fortunate in its topography. On the north and west it is protected by high mountain ranges, and its southern and eastern borders enjoy the advantage of about 300 miles of a magnificent river, navigable and full of fish. The country has two good ports on the Black Sea, Sulina and Kustendje. Along the coast there are extensive sturgeon fisheries.

The Roumanians claim their descent from the colonists of the Emperor Trajan, who conquered the country about 105 A.D., but it is more probable that they did not become a Roumanian people until the thirteenth century. Their language is a Latin tongue, similar to Spanish and Italian, and one third of their vocabulary consists of Slavic and Turkish words. They use the Latin characters instead of Russian and Cyrillian, like their neighbors. Speaking of Latin tongues, it is interesting to note that until about thirty years ago there was a dialect, which was almost pure Latin, spoken by a tribe of people in northwestern Bulgaria.

The Roumanians are very good-looking people, with soft olive skins, beautiful eyes, and a pleasing, agreeable expression, in which they distinctly differ from the sullen-faced Servians. In disposition they suggest the Italian more than any other race that I can think of, being light-hearted, passionate, and pleasure-loving. They do not appear to be much in evidence in trade, nor do I fancy that their talents lie in business capacity. Indeed, the bulk of the commerce of Roumania appears to be in the hands of foreigners.

We were greatly surprised to find a city of such importance, of which we had previously heard so little. I have never seen as many different national ensigns so intermingled in any port of the world, except Constantinople. Port Said and Singapore are lonely compared to it. The only flag I could think of which I did not see was our own, and consequently it was regarded with a great deal of curiosity as we picked our way between the anchored flotillas of barges and steamers.

Close inshore we sighted a flag bearing the name "Istrul Rowing Club," and remembering our kindly reception at Pest headed over for it. On working alongside we saw several oarsmen in rowing clothes about to put a shell in the water. Ranney, who was up forward, hailed one of these, asking if we might make a berth alongside their boathouse.

A well-built, fair-haired young fellow looked at us in surprise.

" Certainly," said he. " But where in the world are you from? "

" London," said Ranney.

The young man smiled.

" No, really," said he, " joking aside, where are you from? "

" I am not joking," said Ranney. " We started from London, and we are bound for Paris via Constantinople and the Mediterranean."

The young man, who was a Dane, looked politely bored.

" But I really am curious to know where you

come from," said he. "Such a boat as that is unusual here."

Ranney showed signs of irritation.

"I tell you we are from London," said he. "I
can't tell you any more. We have come straight
across Europe."

When it became apparent that we were quite
serious there was great excitement. The members
all flocked down and took charge of us in a body.
They detailed a special caretaker for the boat and
carried us up to the Braila Club, a magnificent
building, beautifully furnished. That evening they
gave us a dinner, afterwards taking us for a drive
out to the Casino, later to the theater, and still
later they gave us a supper and reception to which
some of the artistes whose performance we had
previously enjoyed were invited. The party broke
up at about four o'clock in the morning at the boathouse, where certain speeches were made, toasts
given and responded to, and, declining the hospi-
tality of the clubhouse, we went to our bunks, feeling for the first time the somewhat restricted dimensions of the cabin.

Our entertainers represented several nationalities; there were in the party French, German,
Italian, Roumanian, and Danish. All of them

were strenuous business men, for Braila is purely a
commercial city, and most of them were the managing heads of various big industries, milling,
shipping, railroad, telegraph, exporting, etc. In its
prosperous season Braila draws about it the usual
parasites of abundant, quickly acquired gold, and
the theaters and casinos and plazas are gay with
the most cosmopolitan crowd of Europe, while
enormous sums change hands nightly over the
gaming tables in the club.

The following night we gave a dinner to our
thirteen entertainers, and the next morning got an
early start to run the remaining one hundred and
seventy kilometers to Sulina, at the mouth of the
Danube. Before we had gone far the mist closed
down thickly, and for a while it was nervous navigation, as there was a steady stream of traffic;
tows, passenger steamers, and ocean tramp steamers, and the noise of our motor made it impossible for us to hear bells and whistles. After
picking our way cautiously for an hour or so the
fog blew off.

Late in the afternoon the river, now very small,
as we had left the main stream for the narrow cut
which debouches at Sulina, entered a flat, marshy
country, and here, climbing on the top of the cabin

house, I looked across the wild morass and saw the darkening waters of the Black Sea.

Delayed as we were by the fog, the night overtook us before we reached Sulina, but there was no place to pull up, so we lighted our sailing lights and held on. It was very dark when we arrived at the port, and we had some difficulty in picking our way down the crowded quays and finding a berth. Eventually we pulled up at a government landing, where not only were we given permission to lie, but the local authorities even kindly detailed a special policeman to guard the boat during our visit. This was very fortunate, as Sulina is one of the most cosmopolitan ports of the world, and always crowded with vessels of every nationality. The water front is one continuous quay, and the street running parallel, and removed only the width of one row of shallow buildings, is for about half a mile an unbroken line of sailor resorts, dance halls, cafés, theaters, crimp boarding houses, and worse. In spite of all this, the town is orderly and well behaved.

We tied up and went below to put on " shore clothes," thankful at having finished for many weeks with the interminable rivers and canals of Europe. But a casual visitor, when told that we were bound across the Black Sea for Constantinople, remarked:

"Too bad you're so late. The season is changing now; we're due to get an equinoctial gale most any day, and the Lord help you if you get caught in a blow in that thing out in the Black Sea."

CHAPTER XII

WHEN the " floating population " of Sulina, chiefly composed of seafaring folk, learned that we had come " 'cross country " from London in the *Beaver*, and were bound across the Black Sea to Constantinople, we became the object of much friendly remonstrance. They told us that ours was a good sporting proposition for the summer season, but that we had arrived a month too late. It was then the 18th of September; the equinoctial gales were due any day, and with them the seasons changed, and unsettled conditions might be expected thereafter. A thirty-five-foot motor boat all open abaft the cabin house would not last in a Black Sea gale as long as the proverbial snowball in the infernal regions; we had no sail, and, if the motor balked, would drift around indefinitely until we foundered in a gale, were taken off by some passing vessel, or drove ashore to be broken up on the reefs which fringed the greater part of the

222

coast of the Black Sea. All of this we knew to be true enough from our own nautical knowledge and a study of the sailing directions.

It was freely intimated, and has been since, that we were rash and inexperienced. This is not true. Both Pomeroy and I had a full store of sea-going experience in many different types of vessels, large and small. Among my own comparatively recent reminiscences I could recall a hurricane weathered out in Campeche Bay off the coast of Yucatan in a small thirty-ton schooner hove to for three doubtful days, and eventually driven on a lee shore from which we worked off with great difficulty; also a typhoon in the China Sea, much sloppy weather in the Pacific, and a westerly gale on a schooner yacht in mid-Atlantic. There were besides the usual number of minor incidents, such as so many of us have been through who have spent a number of seasons in knocking up and down the New England coast in small cruising boats. Pomeroy had once bought a big English yawl in which he had cruised around the West Indies, and had also a considerable yachting experience in the Mediterranean. Therefore, it can hardly be said that we did not know what we were attempting. People who go down to the sea in big ships very often do not actually know what good weather a small boat can make of an ugly sea if properly handled. Ships' officers themselves have sometimes said to me, pointing over the side when there was a bit of sea on: " What would your little sloop be doing out there now? " And when I answered: " She would be making very much less fuss over it than this tub of yours! " they would look at me with disdain as one who knew not whereof he spoke, while I knew very well that I had been out in much worse weather in some snug little boat without suffering from any anxiety.

No, there was nothing foolhardy in our attempt. We were exposing ourselves to a certain amount of danger, no doubt, but not unwarrantably. Our longest run without a port was only one hundred and twenty-one miles, and the shortest fifty-six. The *Beaver* was a splendid sea boat, full bilged under water, buoyant and capable, and we had traveled for the last two thousand miles without being obliged to stop the motor. Since leaving London we had experienced a great many peculiar and unanticipated dangers, in the Channel, the Seine, and Danube, and we decided that there were, no doubt, a good many more ahead of us in the Black Sea and Mediterranean, all of which were unavoidable details of our somewhat original undertaking to cross and circumnavigate Europe in a thirty-five-foot motor boat. The *Beaver* would have to take her chances with the old Euxine and

Shifting propeller blades at Sulina.

its " hacking waves " just as she would later, after passing out of the Dardanelles, have to do her best with " Levanters," mistral, bora, sirocco, and leveche.

We were fortunate in finding a friend in Sulina. This was Mr. Kuhl, the Chief Engineer of the European Commission for the Navigation of the Danube, with whom Pomeroy was personally acquainted. Mr. Kuhl's courageous years of warfare against the combined forces of the Danube and the Black Sea in keeping the Sulina Channel navigable is very meritorious. We spent an evening at his house, where he showed us in a series of charts the results, and lack of them, of his many years of constant struggle with the great stream, all of which was particularly interesting to me, as only eighteen months previously I had made a study of somewhat similar hydraulic problems at Panama. " Some years I win," said Mr. Kuhl, throwing out his hands, " sometimes it is the river! I make promises, and the Danube breaks them for me, and then the steamship captains swear! " He gave a short laugh. " The Danube flings mud into the Channel, and I scoop it out and build a dike, and make the Danube keep it out. Then the littoral of the Black Sea sweeps it in again, and I make the Black Sea take it away. But this has disturbed the balance, and look! Here is the river filling up the Channel in a single flood, and before I can quell this mutiny there is another somewhere else. Sometimes it has happened that the water has taken charge and flung mud all over the place, and then the steamship captains fling it at the Commission, and they want to know why there is not the thirty feet of water which I promised." He laughed.

It is certainly a man's work, the mastery of such a stream. Mr. Kuhl is about to retire, and I hope that the Commission will get as strong a man to fill his place. They cannot get a stronger.

We lay for two days in Sulina, taking fuel and provisions and getting ready for sea. Mr. Kuhl very kindly rendered us every assistance and had the boat lifted out under the crane of the Commission's yard, where his machinists shipped our spare propeller blades, the old ones which had brought us through several thousand kilometers of river and canals being somewhat scored around the edges. Thanks to the splendid material and construction of the boat and her fine big American elm keel the many bumps which we had given her were scarcely perceptible, but we found a very dangerous state of affairs about the steering gear and one which we did not care to think about in connection with our run through the rapids of the Grein and above the Iron Gate, for the lag-screws holding the iron shoe which took the rudder post had worked loose and were on the point of dropping out, thus leaving the rudder all adrift and the propeller blades unprotected. This was soon remedied, after which we took fuel, a very fine Russian oil from Batoum. We had already taken three hundred and sixty liters of petroleum at thirty cents a liter, but as Mr. Kuhl very kindly let us have the same oil at the wholesale rate paid by the Commission we took advantage of this opportunity and loaded all that we could carry, paving the whole cockpit, engine room and cabin with tins, over which we laid planks to move about on. This was of additional advantage in furnishing us with good ballast, as the boat was too light for open sea, and we should otherwise have had to take on stone or scrap-iron ballast.

We were two days fitting out in Sulina, which time was not lost, as the weather was unsettled and it was blowing hard outside. From the point of land on which Mr. Kuhl's house stood we could see a wicked chop dashing over the breakwater, and a short, steep, combing sea running farther out. We did not object to the delay, as we were in the midst of the most unsettled season, and a day or two lost did not matter. Sulina is a wheat port;

there were a great many vessels loading grain, and the place was full of color and animation. We took our meals in a little restaurant frequented by the captains of tramp steamers—British, German, Austrian, Greek, Italian, Russian, all nationalities in fact—and among these we made a number of friends. The captain of a British tramp, the *Anna Moore*, said one evening:

"Our agent was asking about you chaps today. When I told him you were going to *Constant* in that little motor boat he said: 'Are they crazy?' 'No,' said I. 'They're Anglo-Saxons.' 'But they ought not to be allowed to go!' says he. 'They'll get drowned!'"

We asked him if that was his opinion, and he looked rather grave.

"No," said he. "That's a good sea boat of yours and she ought to make it unless you catch bad luck. It's about two hundred and sixty-five miles to the Bosporus on a straight course. The lightship is fourteen miles off shore. Are you going to lay a course straight across or follow the beach around?"

We told him that it would depend on the weather and how the motor appeared to be running.

ACROSS EUROPE IN A MOTOR BOAT

"If you follow the coast," said he, "you have got á run of eighty miles to Kustendje, then eighty miles to Varna, fifty-six miles to Bourgas, and one hundred and twenty-one miles to the Bosporus. It's longer, but it's safer. You ought to have some sail on that thing."

"Suppose we get a steady glass and good wind and sky?" ,we asked. "Why not make a run direct?"

He shook his head.

"This is the Black Sea, and it's not like anything else. Your glass is no good to you at all. You might have it steady as if it was nailed and the sky without a cloud and a calm sea. First thing you know you'd see a dark streak to the northward. Then *look out!* She's coming down off the Steppes of Russia—a cold slant, and when she hits she'll tear things loose. Have you got a sea anchor?"

We told him that we had not, but thought that we could rig one with the sampan and our anchor. I had done this trick before.

He nodded.

"That boat of yours ought to live through most anything if you can keep her head to sea," he said. "What's your speed?"

"It's supposed to be ten land miles, but it's nearer eight."

He nodded thoughtfully.

"Well, you may just slip in between blows and get it smooth all the way. But if I were to advise you it would be to leave your boat here and come out next summer to finish your trip."

That was the advice we got from everybody, but while we appreciated its value we did not care to follow it, knowing that for many personal reasons if we abandoned our voyage at this time it would be doubtful if we ever finished it.

The boat was all ready the afternoon of the 19th of September, and Pomeroy and I went over to the yard to bring her across to our former berth, intending to start as soon as the weather moderated. It had been raining and blowing, and there was still a good deal of sea running. As soon as we had started the engine Pomeroy suggested that we poke around outside and look it over. We slipped down and headed out through the breakwater, dipping our ensign to a Roumanian man-of-war coming in out of the blow and receiving a return salutation. Once outside we found crazy water due to the hard breeze striking across the eddy made by the river current, but we were both delighted by the behavior of the boat in her deep trim. Throwing in the full strength of the motor we slammed her full bore into and across the ugly rip, through which she went like a trawler, throwing the water freely but perfectly dry.

" We shall not strike it anywhere worse than it is right here on the bar, with this breeze," said Pomeroy.

I quite agreed with him, and we decided to start some time during the night. Running back to our berth we proceeded to take water, after which we got our papers, and said good-by to our friends, in the expectation of leaving before midnight. But a little later there came a big black cloud bank in the north and it began to blow very hard with a cold rain.

By six o'clock in the morning it was still blowing fresh, but the clouds had cleared off and we decided to start, so heating Dan up we ran out through the breakwater, and at seven-thirty rounded the whistling buoy and laid a course for another buoy a couple of miles off shore. Mr. Kuhl had warned us to take a big offing as the sturgeon fishers lay a meshwork of set lines from long trawls all the way from the Sulina Mouth for about thirty miles along the shoal to St. George's Mouth, and it would have been a very serious thing to have whipped up one of these in out propeller.

On passing out from the breakwater we struck a choppy, combing sea, the heavy spray from which gave us a good wetting until we had got off on our course, when we took it astern and it ceased to trouble us.

The Black Sea is almost fresh, receiving as it does the Danube, the Dnieper, the Don, and the Irmak, and of smaller rivers the Dniester, Bug, Kuban, and innumerable others. As a result a fresh breeze quickly produces a short, choppy, lashing sea, which in many places is aggravated by the presence of strong currents, especially along the course which we were taking, where the flow of the three great rivers forms eddies on its way to the entrance of the Bosporus. The terrific commotion caused thereby in a sudden sharp blow gives rise to what are referred to in the sailing directions as the terrible " hacking waves " of the Black Sea.

But the weather, which had at first looked threatening, speedily became glorious. The wind subsided and with it the swell, until by noon we were plowing along in a glassy sea helped on our course by smooth rollers. In spite of our precautions in taking a good offing of five or six miles we several times got among the sturgeon fishers' trawls, but fortunately slid over the set lines without picking any of them up. At ten-five o'clock we passed the first beacon off St. George's Mouth, and a little later slightly altered our course to the westward, as the land drops away on the other side of Dranova Island, and we did not wish to lose sight of it altogether. More than ten miles off shore the Danube water debouching from St. George's Mouth makes a sharp line of color demarcation with that of the Black Sea, the former being an " absinthe frappé " color and the latter a deep sapphire.

Considering the perfect weather conditions we decided not to put into Kustendje, but keeping a good offing to take a departure from the light on Galata Point, and then either cut across the gulf for the Bosporus or lay a course for Bourgas, according to conditions. During the afternoon we lost the land altogether, but picked it up toward evening, and by seven o'clock were off Kustendje and about fifteen miles out.

The evening was a lovely one, the air of a delightful temperature, very clear and the sea like a mill pond. A big school of porpoises came over to play with the boat, and the water was so sparklingly clear and of such a glassy surface that we were able to follow all their movements even when they plunged to their fullest depth. They had not the slightest fear of the noise of the motor, but swam dangerously close to the propeller and frequently rubbed themselves against the sides of the boat. One sportive youngster kept getting across the stem; for almost an hour I lay on my face forward with my head over the bow watching him. He was playful as a puppy and at last invented a little game of his own. Lying across the stem he would let the curve of the bow roll him over and over, presently disappearing to swim back and repeat the performance. I have watched porpoises in many waters of the globe, but have never seen any as kittenish as these.

As soon as the darkness came we picked up our lights, got our position by cross-bearings and laid a course for Bourgas, which would take us about twenty miles off Varna. Dividing the night into two-hour tricks we should have passed it very comfortably had we not been disturbed by the erratic behavior of the motor. In my watch below I was repeatedly awakened by its " missing," but going over it as carefully as I could was unable to find anything wrong, and finally concluded that the trouble had something to do with the lighter quality of the fuel.

Aside from this motor annoyance the night passed uneventfully. A little before midnight the breeze had sprung up freshly ahead, and by three o'clock had kicked up such a head sea that we made very little progress. During my trick at the wheel from two to four I was much puzzled by some peculiar lights flaring up from the sea all about, but on passing closer to one of these I discovered it to be a bonfire on the deck of a good-sized yawl, and was afterwards told that they were built by the fishermen to attract the sturgeon to the set-lines.

At daybreak the wind hauled westerly and began to blow very hard, so that before long the sea was combing nastily and for the sake of getting a lea we altered our course to the westward. The sunrise shone against the flanks of high saffron-colored mountains about fifteen miles away. This was the abrupt end of the Balkan Range which separates Bulgaria and Eastern Roumelia.

" Varna is there," said Pomeroy, pointing to a great rift in the hills. " Shall we put in? "

I answered that on the contrary I should advise
holding straight on our course for Bourgas Bay
and then, if the weather still remained as fine, to
head off straight across the bight for the Bosporus, this last being a run of one hundred and
twenty-one miles. The glass was steady at 30.50,
and the breeze, while strong, was from a good
quarter, but there was a rising, choppy sea which
threw the boat about rather violently, so for the
sake of getting better water we edged in toward
the land.

CHAPTER XIII

TO BOURGAS

T was still early in the morning and Ranney's wheel, when suddenly the forward engine began to " miss," making, at the same time, a peculiar and violent noise, while the speed of the boat was checked by half. A hurried examination of the motor showed that the spiral spring on the forward exhaust valve had snapped, thus putting the forward cylinder out of action, and throwing the entire burden of the work upon its mate.

This was the first accident to any part of the motor which had occurred since leaving London, our early trials being due to defective packing and nuts not hardened down. But although inconvenient and annoying we did not at first regard the situation as serious, having spare parts for practically every part of the engine which was subject to breakage:

On getting out the spare, however, we made a very unpleasant discovery. A comparison with the broken part showed that in order to fit the spring to the valve it was necessary to heat the last spiral, curl it in upon itself and flatten the under surface; in short, a job which needed a forge and a vise to perform. It was also one spiral too long.

We looked at each other in some dismay; the *Beaver* was drifting rapidly out to sea and wallowing violently about on the short, breaking chop which was increasing as we got farther from the land. There was no question of anchoring as we were near the one hundred fathom curve, we had no sea anchor, we were not in the course of any vessel, and the distant peaks of the Balkan Mountains were growing dim.

It is not agreeable to be broken down and blowing off shore in a small motor boat on the Black Sea within one day of the time due for the Equinoctial gales. Although we had made the attempt many times we had never been able to run the motor on one cylinder alone for more than a couple of miles at the most, since to do so interfered with the water circulation, with the result that the cold water all remained in the jacket of the idle cylinder, while the working one quickly heated up, running slower and more laboriously until it finally stopped. When this occurred it was necessary to cool the cylinder before the motor could be started again, and the only immediate way of doing this was to turn it over by hand, a terrific job and requiring perhaps half or three quarters of an hour of the most extreme physical effort. With the breeze off shore and no bottom which we could reach, it scarcely seemed worth while to try to fetch the land on one cylinder, so we set about to see what we could do with the spare spring.

Accordingly, we got out the valve, removed the broken spring, and tried to get the new one in its place. At this point we found that we could not squeeze the spring together enough to adjust it. Using the long clutch-lever to gain power we jammed the spring between it and the after thwart, only to find that when compressed it was barely too long for insertion, and that even if we had got it in we could not have kept it in place against the cap on the valve. As we worked the sea was rising, the boat tumbling about and the spray beginning to wash into the " engine room," as we called the open amidships section occupied by the motor.

" It is no use," said Pomeroy. " We can't fit this thing without a machine shop."

Varna, Roumania.

" How far is Batoum? " asked Ranney, observing our drift.

" About seven hundred miles to leeward. It would be better to try for Varna, which is about fifteen miles to windward."

Poor as it was this seemed to be our only chance, so we jammed down the forward air valves to lighten the work as much as possible for the after cylinder, heated up and cranked the motor. Dan responded sluggishly, and we began to crawl toward the distant Balkan Mountains at the rate of about two miles an hour, bucking a hard breeze and a lumpy sea.

" Do you think you can make Dan do it? " Ranney asked, with a somewhat pardonable curiosity. I told him that I thought so, but he knew that I was not telling the truth. " Suppose he quits? " he asked.

" Then," said Pomeroy, " there will be a salvage job for somebody."

But we all knew that the chances for being picked up were very poor, as the *Beaver* was painted the blue Admiralty " disappearing color " and without any spars or sails.

By plugging the water circulation outlet, which one could do by reaching over the side and then opening the drip cock of the water chamber belonging to the working cylinder, one could somewhat delay the heating up process, as the result was to keep a steady stream of water passing through, where otherwise the circulation was entirely arrested. But the outlet of this stream of water was down into the bilge of the boat. As we had no way of piping it over the side two men were kept busy bailing, one with a pump, a hand affair, the other with a bucket. This was a tedious job, but we were only too willing to keep bailing all day if only the blessed stream would continue to run. Before we had gone far the single cylinder began to show signs of fatigue, and could only be kept at its work by the most careful manipulation of the different controls.

Two hours passed in this way. Ranney would have stopped the motor, when I jockeyed the motor with every resource at hand. At times when we took a big sea full it was necessary to throw out the clutch or the sudden strain on the propeller would have stopped the motor, when I doubt if we could have started it again, as the jacket was so hot that one could not hold one's hand against it. To make matters worse, turning the motor over so slowly and with so little fuel permitted the cooling of the combustion chamber, so that it was necessary to keep the blast lamp going continually, a difficult matter with the wind and spray. Several times we thought that it was finished, and that we were doomed to the fate of a derelict, but each time a careful manipulation of the control brought renewed life to the almost exhausted machine.

Another hour passed, and still the motor pounded wearily on. Standing there watching

17 243

every symptom of failing breath and respiration was like fighting the slow approach of death for the waning life of a man. At times, from some subtle cause, the strength of the motor would flicker up, only to ebb again almost to the point of syncope.

The mountains loomed higher; a mosque, then a slender minaret appeared against the dull green slope far up the bight. Pomeroy and Ranney were almost exhausted from their bailing, so I relieved one of them. As we approached the shore the sea grew quieter and the wind lightened, so that while our power was gradually diminishing our progress was, if anything better. Within three or four miles of the point on the southern side of the bay the motor suddenly stopped. We took a sounding, and finding about thirty fathoms of water, bent our cable to a long towline and got bottom with the anchor.

Thereafter came the laborious job of turning over the engine by hand to get cold water around the hot cylinder, which task fell somewhat solidly upon me, being the only one aboard heavy enough to crank the motor. Ten successive revolutions were all that I was up to without a breathing spell. In time this cooled the cylinder off enough to

A Turkish schooner at Varna.

get the motor going again, and we managed to
work in through blessedly still water almost to the
breakwater, where the engine collapsed again. It
was then getting late in the afternoon, having taken
us all day to work our way in. While lying there
waiting for the motor to cool sufficiently to take
us the rest of the way, a little schooner came in,
flying the Turkish flag, but we noticed that she did
not come from a direction which would have
brought her within sight of us had we completely
broken down.

Our last gasping effort carried us inside the
breakwater, dipping to a Bulgarian man-of-war

as we passed, and within fifty meters of the quay the motor snorted feebly and expired, but our way carried us alongside. Being the first motor boat which had ever been seen in this port, so far as we could ascertain, we were viewed with curiosity and, our American ensign being unknown, with some suspicion. We were too tired to do more than sit in the cockpit and smoke dejectedly, but we handed up our ship's papers and passports to a somewhat peremptory official, who appeared to be the doctor of the port, and told him to kindly take them and clear out and not bother us.

I am afraid that we were more inclined to be disgusted with our hard luck than grateful over being in port instead of flopping around on the Black Sea. Pomeroy and Ranney went below and busied themselves in silence, Pomeroy writing in his log book the following:

and about ten miles from Galata Point the forward engine exhaust valve spring broke, and with great trouble slowly worked our way into Varna. Once we were forced to let go the anchor, and again just outside the breakwater. Get in at 5 and tie up to the quay. Criminal for the engine builders to send a boat to sea with spare parts in such a condition."

246

In regard to this last I will simply make the comment that we were ourselves equally to blame for not having more carefully examined all of these spare parts; still, they looked exactly alike, and one does not dismount one's entire motor for the sake of fitting new parts.

I don't know what Ranney did, but have a strong suspicion that he either whitened his shoes or pressed his trousers with his patent iron.

Eventually I gathered energy enough to rig myself out in a suit of very loud-checked clothes which I brought especially to impress the natives of outlandish parts, and climbed up the quay, where I presently fell in with a beach-comber who directed me to a gentleman who proved to be one of the agents of a shipping house, the head of which, a Herr Hoffmann, we had met in Braila. This gentleman told me that one of their steamers was coming in that evening, and kindly offered to ask his chief engineer to help us.

A little later the vessel arrived, a trim little ship of perhaps two thousand five hundred tons, named the *Kelet*. My new-found friend took me aboard and introduced me to the captain and chief, who were Austrians, and, like all of their nationality with whom I have ever come in contact, kind and

247

courteous. The chief took our spring and spare valve aboard his ship, where he adjusted them, afterwards bringing them aboard the *Beaver* and setting them up.

" If there is any chance of your having trouble with your motor," said the captain, " you had better not try to make the run to Constantinople. If you like I will give you a tow."

I asked him what speed his vessel made, and he told me eleven knots, at which I said that as our steering gear was defective, I did not think that it would be safe for us to tow at that pace through such broken water as we were apt to find outside.

The following morning we started the motor and ran the boat around inside the breakwater, when the behavior of the engine proved far from satisfactory. For some reason both cylinders kept repeatedly " missing "; in the case of the after one I think that this may have been due to our having run it hot for so long a time the previous day, while with the forward one the new valve spring did not fit perfectly and occasionally jammed, throwing the forward cylinder out of its beat, all of which was extremely annoying, the weather being perfect, with a comparatively smooth sea and a bright, cloudless sky.

"Towing behind the *Kelet*."

" You had better let me give you a tow," said
the captain of the *Kelet,* who had witnessed our
difficulties. " I sail in an hour, call at Bourgas
and go on to Constantinople to-night."
Discussing the matter among ourselves, we decided that, considering the bad behavior of the
motor and the trick which it had served us the day
before, we should do better to accept the captain's
offer than to put to sea again under our own power.
If it breezed up we could always cast off and go
our own gait, but as the weather seemed to be
fixed fair it was possible that we might tow straight
through to the Bosporus without encountering any
rough water. Accordingly, we took two towlines
from the port and starboard stern chocks of the
Kelet and a little later steamed out of the harbor
in tow.

Once clear of the bay the steamer headed down
the coast and struck her pace, when we were not
long in discovering that as a barge the *Beaver* was
very far from being a success. Long and narrow
and deep-laden, it was almost impossible to keep
her lined up; she would take a sudden sheer to port
or starboard, then forge ahead like a rope ferry-
boat and could only be brought back with a great
deal of difficulty, a thing which struck us as odd,

for under her own power she ran as true as a die. No doubt we should have done better with a single towline, but once under way we could no longer communicate with the folk on the steamer owing to the roar of water under our bows.

About noon it began to breeze up with the usual nasty, choppy sea, through which we plunged like a porpoise. The constant tendency of the boat to take a sheer caused me a great deal of anxiety, as I knew our steering gear to be very frail, owing to the necessity of carrying the tiller lines through five leads from the tiller to the wheel, and I was afraid that if one of these lines were to suddenly carry away, as had happened many times before, the *Beaver,* deeply laden as she was, would take a side sheer, be dragged on her beam ends, and either fill or roll over before one could reach the tiller or slip the towline. Altogether it was nervous, disagreeable work, with one hand at the wheel and another standing by to grab the helm, and we decided that on reaching Bourgas Bay we would proceed to Constantinople under our own power rather than go through the night with similar conditions.

Halfway to Bourgas the sea became about as rough as we could stand it while being " snaked " through the water at eleven knots. The passengers aboard the steamer were regarding us with great interest, and presently the captain and the chief came aft, followed by one of the hands carrying a basket and a coil of heaving line. The basket was lowered into the water and the line paid out until it came alongside us, making great leaps from the crest of one wave to the next. We grabbed it with our boat hook, hauled it aboard and discovered the contents of the basket to be most excellent Austrian bottled beer.

On arriving at Bourgas Bay the captain of the *Kelet* and I went ashore for a walk about the quaint, semi-Oriental town and along the high bluff overlooking the sea. Bourgas is in Eastern Roumelia on the south side of the Balkan Mountains from Varna, which is in Bulgaria proper. The principality of Bulgaria, which separated from Turkey in 1878, has, like all of the Balkan countries, a very mongrel population, of which at this day scarcely twenty per cent are Turks. The Bulgarians proper are Christians, but do not recognize the Ecumenical Patriarch of the Greek Church, which leads to continual throat-cutting between these dissenting sects, to the damage of their souls and the infinite relish of the Moslem.

" ' Snaked ' through the water at eleven knots."

The Balkan Peninsula and especially Bulgaria present peculiar difficulties to the traveler, the chief of which is the question of language. One speaks Turkish, Bulgarian, Greek, Roumanian, Armenian, Kurzo-Wallachian, Yiddish, with a few dialects which are spoken in Bosnia and Herzegovina, and also those of the Circassians and Georgians. There is also an important language, Serbo-Croatian, which is in fairly common use over the western part of the Peninsula, while the various European tongues are spoken by the more educated people. No three languages would be enough to take one about the Balkans away from the beaten paths. Turkish is the most useful; next to that for the cities, Greek, French, and German, and for the interior, Bulgarian and Roumanian. Of all the European tongues English appears to be the most rare; there are a few American commercial travelers now beginning to filter into the Balkans, but these are usually men selected for their polyglot abilities. Among languages we must not forget the Chingeni of the gypsies.

Bulgaria (ancient Moesia) was the last country to free itself from Turkish rule. Roughly speaking, the area of this principality is a little larger than that of the State of Indiana, but its sanguinary history would be quite sufficient for a country many times its size.

Bulgaria is partly mountainous, partly table-land. From the Danube, which bounds it on the north, it stretches away in a bare, arid plain, rising gently upward to the northern slopes of the Balkan Mountains. On the south side of this range lies the fertile valley of the Maritza, which is shut in on the south by the big Rhodope Mountains, some of the higher peaks of which, Muss-ala and Rila, reach an elevation of 9,615 and 8,790 feet. This range is the geographical separation between Bulgaria and Turkey, and is a wild and impassable region of lofty precipices, high mountain passes, and torrential streams. It was into these fastnesses that Miss Stone, the American missionary, was carried by the Bulgarian bandits who kidnaped her.

Speaking of Miss Stone reminds me of a story which was told me in Constantinople by an English newspaper correspondent who was one of the principal actors. I will relate it just as it was told me.

Miss Stone, it appears, was kidnaped by a band of Pomakes—Mohammedan Bulgarian mountaineers—among whom she was working. These Po-

255

makes, although a Bulgarian-speaking people, are
nomadic and have always followed brigandage as
a profession. They are, in fact, to-day the only
real brigands left in that part of the world. As
the country has become better policed they have
retreated into the inaccessible districts of the Rhodope Mountains, whither it was that they trans-
ported Miss Stone and her companion, demanding,
unless my memory is at fault, a ransom of one
hundred thousand dollars, gold. As there seemed
to be no prospect of obtaining her release in any
other way, the sum was sent from the United
States to the American ambassador at Constantinople with instructions to liberate the missionary.
But here there came a hitch, neither party in the
transaction being willing to trust the other. The
ambassador demanded the custody of Miss Stone
before paying over the money. To this the brigands replied that while they did not doubt the
integrity of this diplomat, yet, considering the
delicate nature of their position and the fact that
it might be unjustly considered one beyond the
obligations of good faith, they must insist upon
getting their money first. In the end they won
their point, holding as they did the trump cards.
There were other large sums of money, but there

was only one Miss Stone. The ambassador, with a chivalry and generosity of which one cannot speak too highly, made himself personally responsible for the amount of the ransom and dispatched two of his attachés to turn over the treasure to the brigands.

But in the meantime every newspaper correspondent in the Levant was on the spot, anxious to be in at the rescue and get Miss Stone's story. The result was so formidable a band that it became obvious to the Americans that they would be unable to keep their rendezvous with the bandits unless they could get rid of the correspondents. In vain they assured the newspaper men that their mission was not to obtain custody of the person of the missionary, but merely to pay over the money, and that the brigands would not release Miss Stone until after the ransom had been received and convoyed to a place of safety. This statement the correspondents received with a wink, considering it a Yankee trick to throw them off the trail.

Thereafter began a game of hare and hounds. The brigands had required that the ransom be brought high up into the hills where there would be no danger of their surprise and capture, and as the guard attached to the treasure was limited to a squad of *Zaptié* or provincial police, it was evident to the Americans that with the formidable array of armed and mounted correspondents it would be impossible to perform their mission. They accordingly tried by all sorts of ruses to shake the correspondents off their trail, but the wily newspaper men told each other that where the gold was there would Miss Stone be also, and accordingly set watches and relieved one another in mounting guard over the treasure box. Disregarding the maneuvers of the Americans they clung like burrs, and so for days this ridiculous chase went on, up and down the country, with false marches here and countermarches there, day and night, while the Americans raged and swore and the correspondents grinned and advised them to send away their escort and " let them in on the game." Miss Stone waited patiently in the little hut high up in the mountains, and her companion nursed her newborn baby, and their Pomake captors fretted and fumed and grew sulky and suspicious.

In the end the Americans had recourse to their Yankee ingenuity. Removing the ransom from its strong box, they filled the latter with stones. Then giving out to the correspondents that they had spoiled the whole affair, they announced their intention of returning to Constantinople the next morning to report that nothing could be done as long as their movements were so hampered. That night the box containing the supposed treasure was stealthily smuggled out of camp, yet not so stealthily but that the keen-scented correspondents got wind of it and followed on its trail. Once they had gone the Americans quickly broke camp, held their rendezvous with the brigands, paid over the money, and returned to Constantinople.

Before long the correspondents discovered that they had been duped, and returned to town, expecting to find that Miss Stone had been rescued and that the laugh was on them. But to their great surprise they learned that the Americans had told them the truth and that there was still no sign of the missionary, at which information they were greatly cheered and decided that the laugh would not be on them after all, but upon the altruistic American ambassador.

A week passed and nothing was seen of Miss Stone. The smiles of the correspondents broadened. Every day a delegation of newspaper men called at the embassy, and the genial query, " Any news of Miss Stone?" assumed the proportions of an insult. Almost a fortnight passed, and then, to the surprise of everybody, including, as my informant claimed, the ambassador himself, Miss Stone and her companion arrived, none the worse for their sojourn among the Pomakes.

The scenery about Kazanlik, on the south slope of the Balkan Mountains in eastern Roumelia, is very beautiful, and the principal industry is a most æsthetic one, being that of the culture of the Damask rose for the extraction of the rose attar. Here the whole countryside is planted in rose trees, the gardens extending high up on the mountain slopes.

The Bulgarian people have made great social strides since their emancipation from Turkey in 1878, and after centuries of cruel tyranny and almost constant warfare their little nation now promises rapid strides in all branches of national life. It has a very well-organized little army of 48,000 men, which in time of war can be expanded to 300,000. Of the whole population, eight and one half per cent are available for military service. Bulgaria, although a poor country taken as a whole, has the reputation of being honest, industrious, and economic. Its educational system is said to be very fine.

The Bulgarian people come of a Finno-Ugric stock and originally emigrated from the region of the lower Volga, entering the Balkan Peninsula in the seventh century, and becoming in the ninth, tenth, and twelfth centuries the dominant race. Thereafter for 500 years they were ground under the heel of Turkish oppression.

Bulgaria is to-day, from a military point of view, a match for any of her neighbors, excepting Turkey. Her infantry is armed with the Austrian Mannelicher rifle and the standard of marksmanship is high. The artillery is supplied with Krupp guns of 1894 model. The cavalry is weak.

Everybody knows more or less about the Siege of Plevna, but few realize what a blood-stained spot this is upon the map of Europe. It was here that Osman Pasha with his army of 50,000 Turks repulsed 80,000 Russians and Roumanians in two big battles fought July 20 and 30, 1877. In December, Osman Pasha led out his whole force in a desperate sortie, which was defeated, when the defenders were obliged to surrender. In the vicinity of the sunny little town of Plevna there are buried nearly 100,000 men who fell in this siege.

Eastern Roumelia is a beautiful country, fertile, green, and fresh, with open, scattering forests and mountains clothed in green to their very summits. Some of these forests are very dense and primeval, and we were told that they abound in game— deer, bear, pig, wolves, chamois—and among the more inaccessible regions a few moufflon. Back in the neighborhood of Philippopolis the great in- dustry of the country is the extraction of attar of roses, and in this region the whole countryside is planted in rose trees of the Damask variety.

But during our brief stay in Bourgas the fea- ture which most interested us in regard to the coun- try was how best to get out of it. Taking coun- sel among ourselves we decided that since we could not trust our steering gear, it was very dangerous to tow behind the *Kelet.* We considered the ad- visability of stopping over a day or two, taking down our motor and giving it a thorough over- hauling, but the objection to this lay in the fact that the weather was apt to change at any moment, when we might be cooped up in Bourgas Bay for days or even weeks before we could put to sea. Eventually we decided that the best course, under the circumstances, was to sail that night for Constantinople, and if, on reaching the entrance of the bay, the behavior of our motor seemed to warrant our going on, to continue. Should it act badly, to return to Bourgas, give it an overhauling, and take our chances on getting a good slant to make our run. There were one hundred and twenty-one miles of open sea from Bourgas to the Bosporus with no port whatsoever between, and we did not think that with the motor running as it was we could make more than about six miles an hour. That meant twenty hours of sea, but by leaving at sunset we counted on being able to arrive at Kavak, get our *firmin* before the sunset gun, and then proceed to Therapia.

Having accordingly decided on this plan we went up to the Custom House, got our papers and cleared for Constantinople. Then as it was growing late we quickly got the *Beaver* ready for sea, little guessing at the tragic fate which lay before her.

CHAPTER XIV

HE sun had disappeared behind the distant peaks of the Balkan Mountains when we heated up the motor, and saying *à bientot* to our kind friends aboard the *Kelet*, cast off from the little steamer and put to sea.

We three aboard the *Beaver* were not a particularly cheerful crew. To begin with we were thoroughly tired out and beginning to feel the strain of our long and precarious voyage. The Equinoctial gales were overdue, it was the 23d of September; we had been repeatedly warned of the suddenness and terrific force of the storms which sweep down from the Steppes of Russia to the northward and lash the almost fresh waters of the Black Sea into a fury where only a very able vessel can live. The *Beaver*, while a good, buoyant sea boat, was not fit for any such ordeal as this; she was entirely open from amidships aft, without any spars or sails, nor did we possess a sea anchor,

264

should it become necessary to heave to. Only two days before our motor had broken down, leaving us almost helpless off Varna, and about fifteen miles out, when we had won our way into the port with the greatest difficulty. Since the accident the motor had been running badly, for we had not wanted to risk losing what might be the last of the good weather in the time spent in overhauling it. Where we should have got at least nine miles an hour out of the boat, we figured that we were getting about six, and we had ahead of us one hundred and twenty-one miles of open sea to the Bosporus, with no intermediate port.

The darkness came by the time we reached the head of the bay, but the night was clear, and although there was no moon it was not dark. Certainly the weather conditions could not have promised greater favor; for three days the barometer had been steady at 30.50; the breeze was soft, southerly and the sky cloudless. If it had not been for our motor trouble we would have anticipated with the keenest pleasure a night run with the expectation of raising the coast of Asia the following day, and a little later entering the famous and beautiful thoroughfare of the Bosporus. Our plan was to call at Kavak to present our papers, and then upon receiving our *firmin,* to proceed to Therapia, where we proposed to lie while visiting Constantinople. Vessels are not permitted to enter the Bosporus between sunset and sunrise, and inasmuch as to ignore this little formality would bring down a broadside from the Turkish forts, it behooved us not to loiter too much *en route.*

Therefore, on reaching the mouth of the bay, with the lights of Bourgas twinkling dimly over the stern, we were very much annoyed when the forward cylinder suddenly stopped work. An examination showed that the new spring which we had adjusted to the exhaust valve had jammed in such a way as to bind the valve, thus preventing its free action, but a little manipulation soon cleared it, and the cylinder resumed its beat. A few minutes later the after cylinder also began to " miss."

" This will not do," said Pomeroy, emphatically. " We have got no license to go to sea in this sort of shape. Let's put back."

Ranney agreed with him and so, theoretically, did I. But, on the other hand, there were certain very strong arguments in favor of going on which I proceeded to point out.

Pomeroy finally agreeing we held on our course. He and Ranney were to take the watch until midnight, when I was to go on until four o'clock. It was then about 8.30, so I went below and had just got to sleep when Pomeroy called me.

"Dan's got a grouch," he said. "We're not doing anything at all."

Dan was certainly limping on both feet, but a little manipulation and a general greasing up soon restored him to good nature. I went back to bed but was unable to sleep, and spent the rest of my watch below listening to Dan's occasional "missing" and making frequent tours of inspection. One of these revealed the pleasing intelligence that the forward cylinder lubrication was choked, and as we did not want to stop the motor, it became necessary to pump the lubricating oil in by hand every few minutes. By midnight I came to the conclusion that we had certainly raised the devil with Dan in forcing him to drive the boat all the way into Varna on one hot cylinder from somewhere off the one hundred fathom line, and that he meant to get square with us if only given half a chance.

About ten o'clock our friend the *Kelet* over-hauled us, passing close aboard to inquire if all was well. As just at that time we were running smoothly we answered in the affirmative, when they wished us good luck and forged ahead on their way to Constantinople. At midnight Pomeroy and Ranney turned in and I took the watch; as the night was fine and the sea smooth the *Beaver*, true boat that she was, ran a straight course, only needing an occasional glance at the compass and touch to the wheel, so that I was able to leave her pretty well to herself and work at the motor, regulating the air-inlet valves and generally going over things, with the result that before very long the engine struck a fairly smooth gait and held it.

We had laid a course from Bourgas straight for the entrance of the Bosporus, and as this coast is excellently lighted, there was never a moment's doubt as to our position, which was fortunate, as it is very easy to miss the mouth of the Bosporus, which has repeatedly happened to big steamers having every facility for holding a true course. The entrance is narrow, about a mile and a half in width I should say, and goes in at an angle to the coast, and as the Asiatic side is high land one cannot distinguish any break in the shore line until close aboard. There is a lightship fourteen miles off shore, but this is not near enough the course from Bourgas for us to have sighted.

At about one o'clock it breezed up ahead, and in half an hour was choppy enough to delay our progress considerably. Toward four o'clock we began to work out across the bight, and when Pomeroy came on deck to relieve me, for we did not think it worth while to wake Ranney, we were well out to sea, and the first vague promise of dawn was beginning to glimmer in the east. The wind had dropped and the stars shone dimly. Pomeroy took the wheel while I went below and, after a glance at the barometer, which was fixed at 30.50, I threw myself down on my bunk and was asleep instantly.

I had been below half an hour when Pomeroy aroused me.

"I don't like the look of things," said he. "Come up and see what you think of it."

I shoved my head up through the hatch and felt a faint, cold draught of air on my face. The sun had not yet risen, but there was a hard light over the sea and a thin gray veil across the sky.

"Look astern," said Pomeroy.

Just over the horizon to the north there was a black streak which appeared to rise as we watched it. It did not seem to be a cloud bank, but was such a blackening as one observes with a hard snow squall, a gray black, quite different in tone from the lurid purple black which brings up a summer thunder storm.

" We are going to have a change of weather," said I.

Pomeroy nodded.

" We are," said he, looking at me anxiously. We both knew what it meant; even if we had not been warned of the fierce gales which sweep down off the Steppes of Russia we would have known. There was a quality in the air, a threat in the cold, thin breeze that warned us of what was coming.

" It is going to blow," said I, " but there's nothing for us to do except to hold on our course. We ought to be pretty near the Bosporus before it strikes; if we're not we will just have to make the best of it. At any rate, I must have some sleep. If it gets bad call me."

I turned in again, knowing perfectly well that there was a fight ahead of us, and wishing to get some rest before it began, as I was thoroughly tired out. But just as I was dropping off Pomeroy called me again.

" Better come up," said he. " It looks rotten."

It certainly did. The thin veil of mist, which was neither haze nor fog, but a high rushing wind, had obscured the sky and was crowding in the horizon. Although we could see for perhaps ten or twelve miles on all sides, there was no land in sight; nothing in fact but gray, steely looking water, with short, angry, breaking waves. We were running before the wind, which blew over the stern with a hard and steady weight. The black line on the horizon to the north had mounted almost to the zenith, but now it had taken the form of a solid blanket of cloud, blown out along its edge in smoke-colored, claw-shaped wisps. It reminded me for the moment of a painting called " The Tempest," in which the gathering storm is represented as a huge black genie, whose vague shape sprawls across the sky, the two clutching hands being alone defined.

The gale overtook us, not in violent squalls, but with a steady and rapidly rising weight of wind, which reared the waves with amazing speed. The velocity of the wind lifted with the same gradual degree, and at the end of an hour was blowing very hard. I would never have believed it possible that a sea could rise to such a size in so short a time; what height the waves actually reached I shall not attempt to say, as I would be sure to exaggerate it, and also because waves are only appalling from their character. The water which we speedily found ourselves in was different from anything which Pomeroy or I had ever seen. We were cutting across a great eddy, formed by the littoral current from the Danube, sweeping around the bight on its way to the Bosporus, and as the water was almost fresh, the sea was straight up and down. In an hour's time it was threatening to break over our stern and fill us up, while at the same time it was breaking back over the bow. A Great Lake sailor might have found himself at home, but it was new to us. As Pomeroy said, the waves flattened out on top and fell back both ways; the terrible " hacking waves," for which the Black Sea is justly dreaded.

Ranney had not awakened, and as there was nothing for him to do we let him sleep. To keep the sea from breaking into the cockpit we had rigged out our heavy canvas side and after awning curtains, which acted admirably as weather cloths. The motor had got over its " grouch " and was running steadily, and for a while the boat behaved so well that we began to have hopes of making the mouth of the Bosporus, which we judged to be about forty miles away.

But presently a new difficulty presented itself. The weather thickened so that we could not see for more than two or three miles, and we began to wonder if we should be able to distinguish the mouth of the Bosporus when we reached it; we wondered also how near we were to being on our course, having run for some hours on dead reckoning and through strong currents, while our compass, although remarkably accurate, must have been to some extent influenced by the motor.

" If we miss the entrance," said Pomeroy, " we are done! There is nothing beyond it but the bald coast of Asia, with never a place to duck in."

I observed that we need not worry about the coast of Asia, as we would never live to strike it. Pomeroy was of the opinion that we ought to edge in and pick up the Turkish coast, but I objected to this on the ground that it was a lee shore. " If we should have to heave to," I said, " we should be in the reefs before morning."

So there we were; off shore we stood a good chance of missing the Bosporus, whereas, if within sight of the land we would not dare to heave to.

As we were discussing the situation we sighted a small brig, hull down, ahead of us, and presently three more, tiny gray blurs through the wind haze. They appeared to be running on a course about two degrees east of ours.

" Those boys are going to the Bosporus," said

I. " The best thing that we can do is to trot along behind them."

" They can't be," said Pomeroy, studying our dripping chart. " They are heading too far to the eastward."

" They have got to be," said I. " There is no other place for them to go."

So we decided to follow them. As a matter of fact we were both right; these little charcoal brigs were running for the entrance, but first they were getting off shore and out of the bad water in the bight before it got any worse.

It was by this time about eight o'clock, and, being very empty, we roused Ranney and asked him to see if he could get coffee and bacon. He came up rubbing his eyes and looking about in bewilderment. Indeed, it must have been a good deal of a shock after turning in of a quiet, peaceful night to " break out " and find the boat in momentary danger of being swamped. He looked inquiringly at Pomeroy and me, and finding us outwardly calm, apparently decided that if we could stand it he could, whereupon he got out the stove, secured it as best he could and set about getting breakfast.

The sea by this time was very bad; we had swung the *Beaver* up so that she took it on her quarter, but she rode as lightly as a big canoe. We were congratulating ourselves on her fine behavior when there came a big comber which broke full on the quarter, flinging the stern bodily out of the water and throwing the boat almost broadside to. There was a shock, a jar, the wheel spun uselessly, showing that the steering gear had parted. I had been expecting this, and jumping aft, clambered along outside the awning stanchions, reached the tiller and managed to swing the boat off before the sea in time to avoid being filled. The wave had knocked the stove clear, flinging our breakfast into the bilge, and as Ranney was trying to rescue the bacon, the parted tiller line was caught in the shaft and immediately wound up. Ranney observing this tore up the cockpit hatch to try to clear it, and I, fearing that he would be thrown down into the machinery and badly injured, began to yell at him to leave it alone. Pomeroy was laying aft to help me, but finding that I could handle the tiller alone he swarmed up forward, and at the momentary risk of being swept off the bow, cleared away the ratline stuff which we had provided for spare tiller lines, and which was at the time in use as an extra lashing for the big anchor. He and Ranney then set about to reeve it in, a very tedious job, as the flooring of the cockpit had to be ripped up and all of the dunnage cleared out of the lazarette. It took about half an hour and was finished none too soon, as it was very difficult to steer by hand with the short iron tiller.

" This will not do," said Pomeroy. " We are not going to be able to run much longer."

The fact was very evident. Every few minutes now there would come a sea which threatened to fill us. We had been obliged to get directly off before the wind, and we did not know exactly how near we were to the land, a bold coast with line after line of reefs between the sea and the beach. Therefore I got forward to rig the sea anchor, which proved to be an awful job and took over an hour to accomplish, as the wind by this time had reached such a velocity that it was hard to work and at the same time keep from being blown off the deck. A difficult detail was getting the big anchor off the bow and lashing it on top of the " sampan " while the sea was playing " diabolo " with the boat, all of which had to be done single handed. The " sampan " itself I rigged in a bridle, so that it would drag broadside on and on its beam ends, and in doing this, as slacking the lashings which held it down was quite out of the question, I was obliged to rig it wrong side before and had a great deal of trouble in getting the repeated turns under and around the boat.

When I looked astern from the bow I wondered how the *Beaver* managed to live. I have spent many weeks on the China Sea and seen some bad water there as well as in the English Channel and the Gulf of Mexico and other seas, but never have I seen such a nasty mess as there was about us. It was only Pomeroy's alert and skillful steering which kept us afloat, and several times as I glanced back and saw a big comber rearing itself over the stern I thought for the moment that it was all up. But each time the *Beaver*, wonderful sea boat that she was, would leap away from under the tumbling water, shipping at the most only a few bucketsful of spray.

The sampan was almost ready when the wind haze ahead thinned out a bit and we caught a glimpse of a bold coast with high cliffs, which appeared to rise sheer from the sea. As we were driving directly upon it we saw that if we hoped to weather out the gale riding to our drag we should have to get more offing. But it was many minutes before there came a patch of water in which we dared try to round up. Even then it was touch and go; broadside on a sea struck the boat and knocked her on her beam ends; she staggered up, and before the next big one hit her was all the way around and nosing her way to windward. For a while we hoped that we were going to be able to poke into it, but before we had got far there came a comber which swept us from bow to stern. The *Beaver* struggled through, hung poised, and then fell into the trough as if pushed off the edge of a wall; the following sea broke across her, but as her weather side was rolled high up she took but little water, the velocity of the wind carrying the bulk of the heavy spray clean across. We came up blinking and gasping and wondering whether we were afloat or foundering.

Pomeroy put his mouth to my ear.

" This is no good! " he shouted. " We've got to heave to! "

It did not strike me that there was much choice, as the reefs were not many miles under our lee. But it was evident that we could not last long as we were going, and there was always the chance that the gale might ease enough to let us start the motor again and work off. So I went forward and drew my knife across the lashings of the drag, and the next sea took the whole thing over the side.

CHAPTER XV

T speedily appeared, however, that owing to her trim and the height of her bow the *Beaver* would not lie head to sea. Instead she took it a little forward of the beam, and seeing that we were in danger of being swept again, we started oiling the sea with the heavy cylinder oil, of which fortunately we had two big five-gallon drums. The effect was wonderful; almost immediately we found ourselves in a patch of big, hurtling seas, the crests of which were barely breaking. A little later the *Beaver*, forging ahead as she rose on a wave, came down across her cable which she snapped like thread, and we were entirely adrift. But as she lay broadside on making good water of the oiled patch, we did not go to leeward much faster than we had before.

For three trying hours we wallowed about in this way, drifting steadily toward the land. At the end of this time Pomeroy, searching the horizon with his glass, made out a lighthouse on a point of land some distance down the coast to the eastward.

" There's the entrance," said he.

It did not seem as if it could be so near, but we had run fast before the gale and it was possible. The outline of the shore was very vague and half hidden in haze, but it was evident that the land put in deeply behind this point.

" We must start the motor," said I.

Pomeroy shook his head. " No use," said he. " The sea is worse than it was. The moment we got outside of this oil patch we should be finished."

Ranney and I did not agree with him, or at least, while not doubting the truth of his words, we thought it better to finish that way than to land up amongst the reefs. By this time we could see what looked like miles of breaking water between us and the shore, so we set to work to start the motor. This proved to be a trying job as the flying water put out the starting lamps as fast as we got them going, and also cooled off the combustion chambers, but by sheltering them with our bodies we managed, after an hour of hard work, to get the engine hot enough to start. During this struggle

Ranney was knocked into the motor by a sea and burned his wrist very badly.

When everything was ready I took hold of the crank and heaved my hardest, but without result. Relieving the compression, I tugged until my joints cracked, but Dan refused to budge. Either the forward cylinder had gripped from lack of cylinder oil, or perhaps there was some other reason; at any rate there was no yielding. The gale was lashing the water across the boat, threatening to douse our lamps and render our work of the last hour futile; every few moments we found ourselves wallowing in a vortex of white, tumbling water. One could not see for the spray driven over the surface of the sea. Those few moments were like a confused and horrid nightmare. It seemed that the one slight chance of saving our lives lay in starting the motor; there was only room for one man at the crank, although Ranney was able to help by getting his feet against the fly wheel. We strained and strained, gasping for breath and blinded by the spume; we shouted to Pomeroy not to be so stingy with his oil; the spray was greasy as it was. Dan at last held us in his soulless power. He braced his ton-and-a-half of heartless metal and defied us. I cursed him and pulled with more strength than was in me, and the only result was that after several minutes of futile struggling I became violently seasick.

The wind was lashing across us in solid sheets of water, and it looked as if we might fill and founder from the spray alone. For the moment I think that we were in the vortex of an eddy. A clumsy, half-blind examination of the motor showed nothing which might help us. I realized fully that the fault was mine in urging that we put to sea without overhauling the motor, after the rough treatment which we had given it working into Varna on one hot cylinder. I do not wish to throw the blame of our position on the engine; a careful or experienced motorist would not have acted as I had, and I knew it.

But regrets were useless; there was apparently nothing left but for us to take our medicine. I flew the ensign reversed and told Ranney to break out the life preservers. I also suggested that as we might possibly reach the shore alive it would be a good plan to secure our valuables, letters of credit, passports, etc. The life preservers were of kapok and very light and soft. As I tied the bands of Ranney's for him he observed with a mournful grin: " When I tried this thing in swimming in the Danube I little thought how soon I'd be wearing it in the Black Sea!"

We took Pomeroy's aft to him and at first he refused to put it on. " I don't mind drowning if I have to," he shouted, for the roar of the wind and the water was deafening, " but I don't intend to be battered to pieces on the rocks!" We had a heated argument with him. "You put it on anyway!" we yelled. "Put it on, do you hear?" We forced it on him, baled him up in it while he growled at such folly. When he had worn it a few minutes he began to grin. "I would have put it on hours before if I had known it was so nice and warm," he said.

As it looked as if we might hit the beach with nothing but the clothes we wore, I went below and shifted throughout, putting on heavy flannels and my most serviceable outer garments. Then being thoroughly tired out and wishing to gain a little strength for the final rub, I wedged myself in my bunk and got about half an hour's refreshing sleep.

Pomeroy called me, shouting that we were getting very close to the reefs. Dead to leeward there was a strip of sandy beach, and behind it a low building which looked like a boathouse. In the hope of attracting attention, I fired several

283

shots from our gun, which sounded like a popgun in the blast of the rushing wind. As we drifted farther in it looked as if the breakers directly in shore were less violent than on either side, and it occurred to me that if we could only get the boat off before the wind with some steerage way, we might perhaps be able to beach her.

But there was no time to lose, so I yelled to Pomeroy to rip off the side awning curtains, as these kept the stern from swinging to the wind. He whipped out his knife and slashed them free, and at the same moment I put the helm hard up. The gale caught our high bow and swung her off; heavy sprays swept across the stern, but we began to gather way, and a moment later we were scudding at good speed through a smother of breaking water. Yelling to Ranney to take the wheel I got out our second big drum of lubricating oil, uncorked it, and holding it across the gunnel let it run full bore, about an inch and a half stream into the sea. The effect was quickly evident; as the big combers hurtled past their crests, instead of curling high and breaking, crumbled off in boiling masses of yellow spume. Before we reached the outer reef there was a big oiled patch astern of us.

" Here we go   ! " yelled Pomeroy, and
the *Beaver* leaped forward into the moving water.
A wave crashed against the stern and drove us
ahead like a maul; the next instant we were in a
roaring, leaping, spouting chaos of breakers which
tossed the boat in air and spun her around as if
she had been a toy, yet driving her always furiously ahead. Cascades of spume came tumbling
aboard, but the buoyancy of the boat kept her
above the solid water. All about us the surf
seemed to be a lashing maelstrom of yellow froth.
Everything was greasy, but the drum of oil was
nearly empty. Ranney, clinging to the wheel, was
unable to keep his footing; once he fell, and the
boat started to broach to, but he clung to the
spokes, and Pomeroy reached down and grabbed
the wheel with him, straightening us out before
the next sea broke. It looked to me as if any following sea might roll us over, and I yelled at them
to jump back to windward if she filled; otherwise
they would have been rolled under her, and either
crushed on the rocks or drowned. My drum of
oil ran empty, so I threw it overboard and reached
around to take the wheel, shouting at Ranney to
get out from under the awning stanchions, and I
remember being furiously angry when he merely

grinned and shook his head and yelled: "All right! All right!"

Pomeroy kept shouting: "No! No! Hold on! Not yet! Not yet!"

Oddly enough there was nothing at all terrifying about this part of it. After the hours of cold and helpless inertia in waiting for what we thought would be certain death it acted as a stimulant and seemed to bring back all of our force. It was wild, exhilarating, tremendous, like the rush of a racing automobile, or a cavalry charge, or artillery going into action. Twice the crumbling crests of the breakers came boiling over our stern, but the good, stout canvas held and kept us from filling. The uproar of the sea was deafening; we were all howling together at the top of our lungs, and when we saw that we were through the worst of it we began to laugh and shout. Almost ashore we came down with a crash upon a reef, knocking a hole the size of one's head in the starboard bilge, but so great was the drive of the following sea that we did not sink.

Suddenly from the long, low building behind the beach there came running a gang of swarthy men, half naked, with huge bulging muscles and red fezes on their heads. They were carrying a

"A sea broke under the boat and flung her up on the beach."

surf line, and out into the breakers they came, squattering through the surf like a pack of retrievers. But when they saw that we were racing ashore in style and needed no help they fell back upon the beach, shouting.

In we drove. We grounded. A sea broke under the boat and flung her up on the beach. The next sea threw her higher. The Turks rushed out in the water, caught a turn on the samson post with their surf line and hove ahead. We splashed out waist deep, scrambled ashore and lent a hand. A wave broke into the boat and we suddenly thought of our duffle. A line was quickly formed, the stuff handed out, baled up in our blankets and carried back from the beach. In ten minutes the *Beaver* was filled chock-a-block with sand.

It appeared that we had driven ashore directly in front of the last station to the westward of the International Life Saving Service at a place called Darboz, and the only spot for many miles, as we afterwards learned, where we could have won our way to the shore alive. The building on the beach was the boathouse; the station was at the top of the hill, and thither we were conducted by the *umbashi* or coxswain of the life savers. There was also a Turkish military guard quartered there, and

the lieutenant in command, who was not over intelligent, confiscated our effects and gave us to understand that we were prisoners. In his eyes our
gun and cartridges made a very bad case against
us. When I attempted to take some photographs
immediately on landing he tried to interfere, but I
posed him in front of the camera and took his picture before he knew just what was up.

The Turks could not make us out at all, as they
did not know a word of the five languages with
which Ranney spattered them. We proceeded to
make ourselves at home in the station, and the life
savers, who are a magnificent corps, were very kind
and hospitable. They gave us dry clothes and
brandy and tobacco, and made us hot tea and offered us such food as they had, which consisted of
bread, olives and onions.

It was getting dark; we could not find out where
we were nor how far from civilization, but it was
evident that we had landed in a very wild and savage country, utterly uninhabited and remote. Back
of the cliffs there was a patch of sandy desert, with
distant forest-covered hills and a lake two or three
miles long. Ranney finally made the *umbashi* understand that he wished to send a note, and accordingly wrote out a brief statement of our condition

which he addressed to the American ambassador at
Constantinople, with whom he was personally acquainted.

We were given comfortable beds at the station,
and the next morning Captain Russell, an Englishman and the chief of the International Service, arrived from his headquarters, the station at Kilios,
at the entrance of the Bosporus. Captain Russell
told us that the messenger with our dispatch had
arrived at Kilios, a little tramp of twenty-three
miles, at two o'clock in the morning. The man
had been unable to describe the *Beaver,* but said
that it was similar to a lifeboat, having neither
sails nor steam nor oars, and propelled by " something alive " inside it. Captain Russell had set off
immediately on horseback, and had ridden all
through the tempestuous night, arriving at our
station, which was at a point called Darboz, at
8 :30 A.M. Part of the way the trail led along
the beach, and as the gale had driven the water in
he had once or twice been obliged to ride through
the surf.

Captain Russell told us a great many interesting stories about the International Life Saving
Service. Under his direction were the five stations
on the European side of the Bosporus, of which

the one at Darboz where we had arrived was the last. All of his crews were natives, and a more splendid corps it would be hard to find. These men are picked for the most part from the fishermen and sailors all along the coast, a strong, hardy race of people, and those who are chosen pass through a very severe competitive examination of proficiency. The average life saver looked to be nearly six feet in height, tremendously boned and muscled, with legs like a wrestler and a chest like a bosun's mate. The candidate is required to swim out through the surf in all of his clothes, or is perhaps told to jump overboard and swim ashore when out in the lifeboat some day in midwinter, with half a gale blowing on to the beach and the thermometer well below freezing. He must be an expert in rope lore and able to throw any kind of a hitch without stopping to think. Also his general intelligence must be up to a certain grade and he must be a man of good moral character, which, indeed, all of the people of this class appear to be. Sometimes Captain Russell will take several applicants a mile to windward, with a blizzard raging, and then have them jump overboard and swim a race to the beach, promising the billet, other things being equal, to the first man ashore. Considering the strenuousness of these trials one would hardly think that there would be many applicants for the billet, but as a matter of fact the position of life saver, although the pay is very slight, is most eagerly coveted. Your Turk desires of all things a salaried position, which is generally regarded in the community as a token of worth and responsibility, and in the case of the life savers it certainly is such.

But even after the candidate is accepted his life is far from being a primrose path. Aside from the hardship and danger of the service, especially in the winter when ship after ship is coming ashore, Captain Russell works his crews at every sort of drill imaginable, for the most part in the summer months, as the winters are very severe, the climate of the Black Sea being similar to that of our coast around Cape Cod. One of the drills is to take a lifeboat crew out when there is a big surf, let the boat broach to and roll completely over with all hands aboard. As the boats are self-righting and self-baling, they come up on an even keel again, while the men are supposed to cling to their thwarts, coming up with the boat when she rights.

Captain Russell told us that one night in mid-winter, with a hard snowstorm raging, he received news that there was a vessel ashore between two of the stations, Darboz and Kara Burnu. On reaching the spot he found a big Russian emigrant ship, with a cargo of Crimean Jews for New York, piled up on the reef a couple of hundred meters from the shore. There was a terrible surf running, and the conditions being more favorable for operating the breeches buoy, he decided to take the people off in that way. He himself got aboard the vessel with some of his men, the rocket was fired from the shore and the apparatus rigged from the vessel's fore truck. The poor emigrants had to get up the rigging and into the buoy, which they accomplished without any accident. We asked Captain Russell if they did not have a good deal of difficulty in managing this part of the programme.

" No," said he; " the only trouble we had was in separating them from their personal effects. One Polish Jew came ashore in the buoy with a big black trunk in his arms. How he got it up the rigging to the masthead and then into the buoy beats me. He must have tied it on his back and crawled up the best way he could. There was a blizzard blowing, with the wind about ninety miles an hour."

Among the women who came ashore there was one who, Captain Russell decided, would probably become a mother before morning, but after she had been comfortably established in one of the rooms usually reserved for officers, this impression was discovered to have been due to an enormous loaf of Russian bread with which the good woman had provided herself against the exigencies of shipwreck.

Captain Russell had his hands full with the three or four hundred emigrants taken off this ship. It was in the middle of winter, the ground being deep with snow, the weather tempestuous, and no communication except by horse or camel to Constantinople. The station could only accommodate about one hundred people, so big tents were erected, the food supply of the vessel brought off in the lifeboats, and a well-organized refuge camp was established and maintained for some weeks until the castaways could be disposed of.

It is not at all uncommon for three or four ships to come ashore in the same gale, owing to the treachery of the currents, the terrific wind and sea, and the ease of missing the Bosporus En-

trance. After we had heard a few of these tales
we did not feel so chagrined at being tossed up
on the beach in the poor little crippled *Beaver*.
Captain Russell told us that during one winter's
gale there had been ten vessels ashore between
Kilios and Darboz in a single night.

Among other anecdotes, Captain Russell told us
that early in the summer the Italian ambassador
to Turkey had come around from Constantinople
in his steam yacht to visit the station at Kilios.
The ambassador was highly delighted with everything which he saw, and returning aboard his
yacht with Captain Russell, said that he wished
that some day he might be able to see the operation of the breeches buoy.

"If you like," said Captain Russell, "I can
send you ashore in it now."

The ambassador looked a little startled and replied that while he would much enjoy the demon-
stration he was not particularly anxious to be the
principal actor.

"Then," said Captain Russell, "perhaps you
would like to see me send one of your sailors
ashore?"

"That would be very interesting," said the
ambassador.

"It is possible," said Captain Russell, "that we may knock your funnel down."

"Oh, never mind the funnel!" said the ambassador, who was a good sportsman.

Accordingly, Captain Russell signaled to the lookout, and a few minutes later the rocket came soaring between the two masts of the yacht, and without striking the funnel, went into the sea on the other side. The crew quickly hauled in the line and rigged the gear from one of the masts, when a sailor jumped into the breeches buoy and was hauled ashore, to the great delight of the ambassador.

There is a similar branch of the International Life Saving Service, under another chief, also an Englishman, on the Asiatic side of the Bosporus.

We spent three days at Darboz trying, with the assistance of Captain Russell and a big crew of his men, to get the *Beaver* high up on the beach, where we might be able to repair her and float her off again. The boat had been badly mauled. Her seams were sprung, her cabin house was shifted, there was a hole punched in her side, and some of her frames were broken. Working hard for three days with a trained wrecking crew, stout gear, and two yoke of buffalo, we were unable to get her out

"In the end we accepted an offer for the wreck."

of the hole into which she had settled. No doubt we could have done so as soon as the gale abated entirely and the water stopped settling her in the sand, but the whole job promised to be lengthy and expensive. We did not see how we were going to float her over the reef where we had come in, and also we were a month behind our schedule, and by the time we were ready to go on the season would be too far advanced for us to hope to finish our voyage. In the end we accepted an offer for the wreck made us by Captain Russell.

The day after we had come ashore the Turkish military commandant of the *vilayet* called upon us and left instructions that we were to be treated with every courtesy. Your genuine Turk who is not corrupted by metropolitan life is an exceed-ingly admirable person, being honest, temperate to the point of abstemiousness, scrupulously clean in his person, deeply and honestly religious, and of a kindly, cheerful, but dignified disposition. I have never seen more splendid physical specimens of men than the life savers and the fishermen along the coast of Turkey bordering on the Black Sea. The life savers were as curious as children, and tremendously interested in all of our little effects. The whole crew assembled to see Ranney shave

Salving the motor.

Bernard Williams

299

himself with his safety razor, following the process with grave faces and little clicks of admiration. They implored me to play them a tune on my little typewriter, and when they discovered that it was not a musical instrument, but a writing machine, they were charmed, and every man jack of them begged to operate it. When we unpacked our things they clustered about, picking up each little object, and passing it from hand to hand, but always returning it to its place. Not a thing was stolen by this corps, but I cannot say as much for the soldiers, who were a low-grade mongrel lot of conscripts.

The station was located in a very malarious district, and most of the men were suffering from fever. As I had saved the medicine chest, which was well stocked with quinine, arsenic, calomel, etc., I was able to treat all hands and to leave them well supplied with the necessary drugs. One old fellow, in whom I diagnosed a serious intestinal condition, told Captain Russell that Allah had cast the American doctor upon the shore in answer to his prayer that his life might be saved. Perhaps he was right. Ahmed himself had saved many a life from the Black Sea, and I like to think that his God may have used us as an instrument for bringing his succor from the same source. The loss of a motor boat is not a high price for the life of a brave man, and as Captain Russell told me that he would have Ahmed removed to the hospital, it is possible that the prayer of the Turk has been answered.

Our friend the *Kelet* tried to send a vessel to our aid, but no one would venture out. This we learned afterwards from Mr. Kuhl.

And so ended ingloriously our ambitious undertaking. The *Beaver* was not insured, so there is no chance of our attempting to finish our voyage. The beach was strewn with our many effects. I picked up one of the sidelights two hundred yards from where we struck; the sampan, the little boat which we had built in Pomeroy's studio on the *Rue des Sablons*, we found miles down the beach, stove to pieces. It was a sad sight to see our little domestic belongings scattered here and there along the water's edge, soggy and full of sand. Everything had washed out of the cockpit, including a very fine compass and my new marine glasses. Ranney was disposed to criticise us for bewailing our property when we should have been grateful for having saved our lives, but the *Beaver* and everything aboard her, except Ranney, belonged to Pomeroy and me, and represented many months of hard work and preparation; besides this, there is always a certain melancholy about the shipwreck of a boat aboard which one has lived for some time.

But such is the luck of the sea, so we loaded what duffle we had saved into an *araba* drawn by buffalo, and set out on our overland journey for Constantinople. The country which lay between was very wild and there was no road, so we were obliged to follow the beach around. With Captain Russell as our guide we made the first day's journey on foot, winding between the sand hills and along the cliffs to the next station, at Kara Burnu. This was the point which Pomeroy had taken for the Bosporus entrance, as many, many navigators have done before to their doom. It marks what is known as the " False Entrance," and has been the death trap for many a vessel. Indeed, this whole coast is an exceedingly dangerous one. Captain Russell told us that he has had ten big ships ashore in a single night. Fortunately, the International Life Saving Service is a remarkably efficient one; its splendid work would require volumes for the telling.

Our second day's journey, on horseback, brought us to Kilios, whence we rode across some beautiful

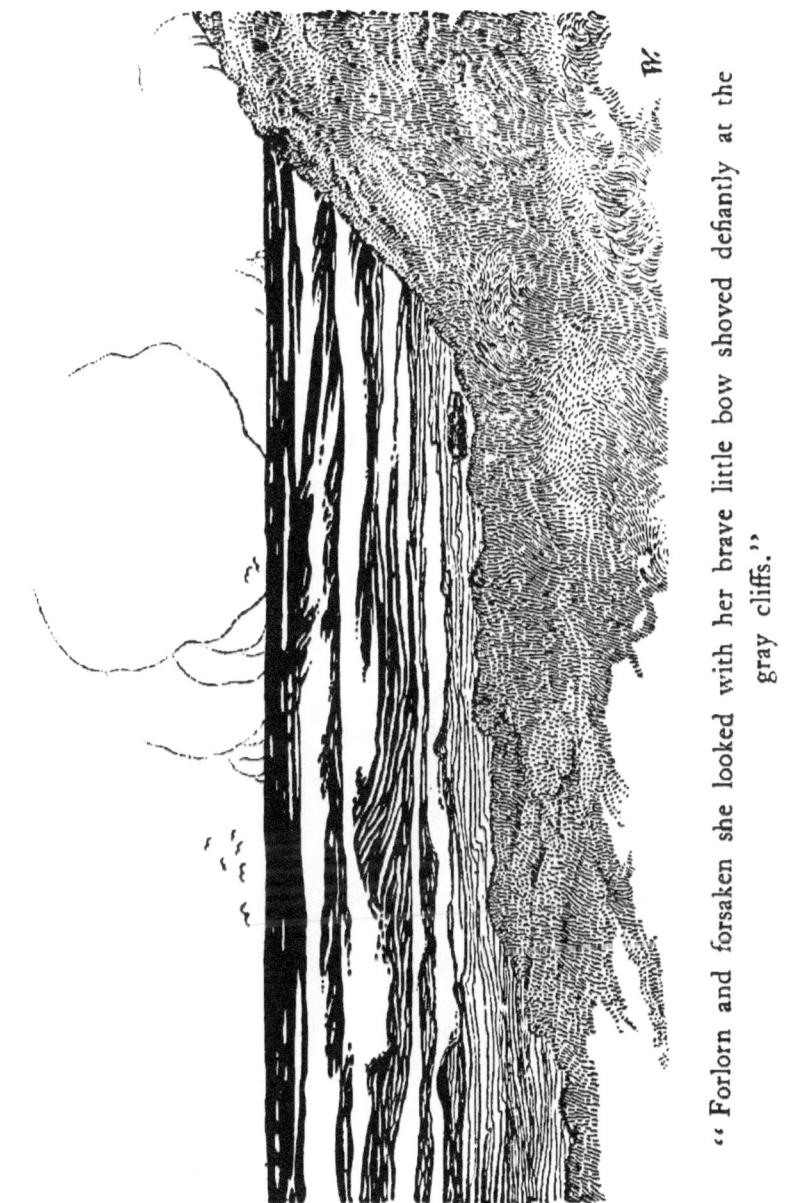

" Forlorn and forsaken she looked with her brave little bow shoved defiantly at the gray cliffs. "

ACROSS EUROPE IN A MOTOR BOAT

country to the Bosporus, where we caught a boat for Constantinople.

But our farewell to Darboz was a sad one. Far down the lonely beach we turned for a last look at the little *Beaver,* a small, blue streak at the water's edge. Forlorn and forsaken she looked with her brave little bow shoved defiantly at the gray cliffs, while the swirling water dug her sandy grave.

An honest little boat, she put up a plucky fight against heavy odds, and saved the lives of those who trusted in her, even though it cost her own.

(1)

THE END

www.ingramcontent.com/pod-product-compliance
Lightning Source LLC
Chambersburg PA
CBHW021405110726

47901CB00008B/2069